ABSOLUTELY HILARIOUS ADULT GOLF JOKE BOOK

A Treasury of the Best Golf Jokes Causing Loud Guffaws and Laughing Convulsions.

Hilarious Golf Jokes For The Clubhouse Bar, On The Course, Backups at the Tee or any time.

Presented by The Team at Golfwell.Net
www.golfwell.net

Absolutely Hilarious Adult Golf Joke Book

Praise for Absolutely Hilarious Adult Golf Joke
Book

"A f%$#ing gut buster!"
J.J. Kansas City

"Instead of getting pissed at the slow players in
front, pull this book out a have a laugh."
B.R. Ponte Vedra Beach, Florida

"Can't put it down…. After reading it, I'm not so
serious on the course anymore and I play better
relaxed."
T.W. Los Angeles

This book is dedicated to golfers everywhere - whether you're one of the best that ever was or one of the worst that ever was – we just want you to enjoy the game and laugh. You will play better too!

We collected and organized these jokes over the years. You may have heard variations of these jokes but all of them are golf related to get into this book. They are absolutely the best compilation of the best adult golf jokes around. Enjoy!

1. CELEBRITY GOLF JOKES

Donald Trump and Ted Cruz are standing at the first tee and their caddies walk up. The caddies look at each other very impressed and the first caddy tells them, "Wow! This is an honor to be able to caddy for you fine gentlemen. Why did you come to play our course today?"

"We're planning WW III," says Senator Cruz.

"Really," the other caddy says. "What's going to happen?"

Trump says, "We're going to kill 140 million Muslims and one blonde with big tits."

The other caddy says, "A blonde with big tits? Why kill a blonde with big tits?"

Trump turns to Cruz and says, "See, I told you, no one gives a shit about the 140 million Muslims."

"Hey doll. Could you scare up another round for our table here? And tell the cook this is low grade dog food. I've had better food at the ball game, you know? This steak still has marks where the jockey was hitting it."

-Rodney Dangerfield, Caddyshack

John Daly walks into the clubhouse bar and reads a sign that hangs over the bar:

FREE BEER! FREE BEER FOR THE PERSON WHO CAN PASS THE TEST!

So John asks the bartender what the test is.

Bartender says, "Well, first you have to drink that whole gallon of pepper tequila, the WHOLE thing at once and you can't make a face while doing it. Second, there's a 'gator out back with a sore tooth...you have to remove it with your bare hands. Third, there's a woman up-stairs who's never had an orgasm. You gotta make her have one and make things right for her."

John says, "Well, I've done some outrageous things in my life, but as much as I would love free beer, I won't do it. You have to be nuts to drink a gallon of pepper tequila and then it gets crazier from there."

Well, as time goes on John drinks a few, he asks, "Wherez zat teeqeelah?" He grabs the gallon of pepper tequila with both hands, and downs it with a big slurp and tears are now streaming down his face.

Next, he staggers out back and soon all the people inside hear the most frightening roaring and thumping, and then silence. John staggers back into the bar, his shirt ripped and big scratches were all over his body.

"Now" he says "Where's that woman with the sore tooth?"

"There are probably some things I could do to keep my flexibility up, but I'd rather smoke, drink diet Cokes and eat."

-John Daly

John Daly is shopping for a new motorcycle. He finally finds one for a great price, but it's missing a seal, so whenever it rains he has to smear Vaseline over the spot where the seal should be or else it won't start.

Anyway, his girlfriend is having him over for dinner to meet her parents. He drives his new cycle to her house, where she's outside waiting for him. "No matter what happens at dinner tonight, don't say a word." She tells him, "Our family had a fight about doing dishes three days ago. We haven't done any since, but the first person to speak at dinner has to do all of them."

John sits down for dinner and it is just how she described it. Dishes are piled up to the ceiling in the kitchen, and nobody is saying a word. So John decides to have a little fun. He grabs his girlfriend throws her on the table and fucks her in front of her parents. His girlfriend is a little flustered, her dad is obviously livid, and her mom horrified. John smiles and sits back down, but no one says a word.

A few minutes later John grabs the mother, throws her on the table and fucks the hell out of the mother. Now his girlfriend is furious, her dad is furious and about to lose it all, but the mother is a little happier. But still there is complete silence at the table.

All of a sudden there's a loud clap of thunder, and it starts to rain. John remembers his motorcycle outside in the rain. He jumps up and grabs his jar of Vaseline. Upon seeing this, the father backs away from the table and screams, "Okay, that's enough! I'll do the fucking dishes!"

"Somebody made the statement that Donald Trump has built or owns the greatest collection of golf courses, ever, in the history of golf. And I believe that is 100 percent true."

-Donald Trump

Tiger Woods went into a Spanish bar and sat down next to Sergio Garcia who was chewing gum. Sergio, in between chews, said, "You Americans think you're so great."

"No, we're just like anyone else," Tiger replied. "I enjoy Spanish food very much, especially paella."

Sergio sneered, "Ha! You Americas are too fat! You eat too much bread."

"Oh yes, we love to eat bread," replied Tiger. "Of course, we eat the inside of the bread and take the outside and recycle it then make cereal with it for Spain."

Sergio, still chomping away on the gum asked, "You Americans eat too many bananas like the monkeys."

Tiger still cool replied, "Well of course we eat bananas and recycle the peels and make smoothies for Spain."

Sergio, still chewing away and clicking the gum, "I hear you are a sexual experto. But Americans do not know how to have good safe sex."

Tiger unfazed, said, "Oh yes, we use condoms for sex and when we finish with them we recycle them and make gum for Spain".

"I'm not saying my game of golf went bad, but if I grew tomatoes, they'd come up sliced."

-Lee Trevino

Sergio Garcia, Jack Nicklaus and Arnold Palmer are standing before God at the throne of Heaven. God looks at them and says, "Before granting you a place at my side, I must first ask you what you believe in." Looking at Nicklaus first he asks, "What do you believe?"

Nicklaus looks God straight in the eye and says, "I believe the game of golf to be one of the joys in life. It brings happiness and good times to so many people as well as business opportunities. I was fortunate to be able to play well and devoted my life to bring such joy to many people. I don't have any regrets." God offers Nicklaus the seat to his right.

God then turns to Arnold, "And you, Mr. Palmer, what do you believe?"

Palmer stands respectfully, "I believe courage, honor and passion are the fundamentals to life and I've spent my whole playing career

providing a
living embodiment of these traits. Like Jack, I
too was very fortunate to be able to play well
and influence more people to enjoy the game."
God, moved by the passion of the speech offers
Arnie the seat to his left.

Finally, he turns to Sergio. "And you, Mr.
Garcia, what do you believe?"

I believe..." says Sergio "... that you're sitting in
my seat."

"Oh this is your wife, huh? Hey baby you musta've been something before electricity."

-Rodney Dangerfield, Caddyshack

Ernie Els died and was up before God for Judgment. He was met by St. Peter at the Gates of Heaven who greeted him. "Mr. Els, you were a great golfer but before you meet God, I thought I should tell you that other than your great golf career, you really didn't do anything for the common good or for the bad, so we're not sure what to do with you. We don't have any golf courses in heaven but what particularly did you do on earth that was good?

Ernie pondered for a bit and said, "Once after playing a golf tournament in California, I was driving back to the hotel and there in the parking lot, I saw a young woman being tormented by a group of Hell's Angels – you know revving their engines, circling her, taunting her with obscenities?"

"Go on," said St. Peter.

"So I stopped and got out of my car with my 5 iron and went up to the leader – the biggest guy there. He was much bigger than I, very muscular, had tattoos all over, a scar on his face and a ring in his nose. Well, I put my index finger in his nose ring and tore it out of his nose. Then I told him and the rest of them they'd better stop bothering this woman or they all would get more of the same!"

"Wow, that's very impressive Ernie!" St Peter replied. "When did this happen?"

"About two minutes ago," said Ernie.

"I was a pitcher, and my dad played in college. The hardest day of my life was telling him I was going to quit focusing more on golf. But with golf, I felt like the game can't be perfected, and that motivated me."

-Jordan Spieth

Jack Nicklaus had many current PGA golfers for a BBQ around a small beautiful lake at his North Palm Beach estate. He announced a contest to all of them. If any person present dared to swim across the lake, the successful swimmer would win $10,000, or instead of the money, Jack would share his golf secrets and his secrets to keep a good mental attitude and maintain discipline during a round which enabled him to win more majors than any other golfer. But Jack first told everyone there were 10 hungry alligators in the pond.

After a period of silence, all watched as Sergio Garcia suddenly splash into the lake and began swimming like hell! He was swimming so fast it looked like he was running on top of the water, throwing up a hell of a wake!

After crossing the lake and climbing out breathless just ahead of several gators rapidly closing in on him, he laid a safe distance away on the ground dripping wet and completely exhausted. The others gave him a thunderous applause!

Jack, amazed at Sergio's bravery, couldn't believe it. He congratulated him and then asked what do you want $10,000 or his secrets to winning majors?

Sergio replied, "Let's start by finding out the motherfucker who pushed me in. That was you, Woods, wasn't it, no?!"

"Hockey is a sport for white men. Basketball is a sport for black men. Golf is a sport for white men dressed like black pimps."

-Tiger Woods

Rory McIlroy initially met Caroline Wozniacki in a bar. They talk, they connect, and they end up leaving together. Caroline takes him back to her place, and as she shows him around her apartment, Rory notices that her bedroom is completely packed with teddy bears. There were hundreds of small bears on a shelf and all the way along the floor, medium sized ones on a shelf a little higher and huge bears on the top shelf along the wall.

Rory is surprised that Caroline would have a collection of teddy bears, especially one that's so extensive, but he decides not to mention this to her. Rory turns to her... they kiss... and then they rip each other's clothes off and make love. After an intense night of passion, and as they are lying there together in the afterglow, Rory rolls over and asks, smiling, "Well, how was it?"

Caroline says, "You can have any prize from the bottom shelf."

"The more relaxed you are, the better you are at everything, the better you are with your loved ones, the better you are with your enemies, the better you are with your job, the better you are with yourself."

-Bill Murray

It's 1963, Jack Nicklaus is playing the final hole at The Masters on his way to his first Green Jacket. He hits a three wood just short of the bunker on the left side of the fairway and as he and his caddy are thinking over his next shot, Jack notices a snail going slowly past his ball. Not wanting to hurt the snail, he gently picks it up and walks over to the trees on the right side of the fairway and flings it into the woods.

It's now 1986, and Jack is again playing the final hole at Augusta on his way to winning his record 6th Green Jacket. While he and his caddie are looking over his second shot he sees a snail by his golf ball. He bends down to pick up the snail and it's the same snail from 23 years ago. The snail creeps half way out of his shell, looks at Jack and says, "What was that for?"

"If you think golf is relaxing, you're not playing it right."

-Bob Hope

Tiger Woods just finished playing the Emirates Golf Course in Dubai and met a very beautiful virgin woman – more beautiful than any woman he'd ever seen in his life. He persuaded her to cross the desert with him to a secret hideaway where they could escape the crowds.

They rode a camel across the desert but on the way there, the camel suddenly dropped dead. After dusting themselves off, they solemnly pondered their situation. After a long period of silence, Tiger spoke. "Well my dear, this looks pretty grim."

The virgin replied, "I know, in fact, I don't think it's likely that we can survive more than a day or two."

Tiger replied, "I sadly agree, my dear. Since we are unlikely to make it out of here alive, would you do something for me?"

Yes, anything," she said.

"I have never seen a virgin's breasts and I was wondering if I might see yours?"

"Well, under the circumstances I don't see that it would do any harm." She opened her gown and Tiger enjoyed the sight of her shapely breasts, amazed at their beauty.

Tiger continued, "My dear, would you mind if I touched them?"

She blushed but consented and he fondled them for several minutes. Then the young virgin spoke, "Tiger, could I ask something of you?"

"Yes anything."

"I have never seen a man's penis. Could I see yours?"

Tiger thought for a second then said, "I supposed that would be OK," and he quickly took off his pants.

"Oh Tiger, may I touch it?"

"Oh yeah," Tiger said.

After a few minutes of fondling Tiger was sporting a huge erection. "My dear, you know that if I insert my penis in the right place, it can give life."

"Is that true Tiger?"

Tiger smiled and said, "Yes it is, my dear."

"Then why don't you stick your dick up that camel's ass and let's get the hell out of here."

On Jim Furyk's swing: "It looks like a one armed man trying to wrestle a snake in a phone booth."

-David Feherty

On a golf tour in Ireland, Tiger Woods drives his BMW into a gas station in a remote part of the Irish countryside. The pump attendant, obviously knows nothing about golf, greets him in a typical Irish manner completely unaware of who the golfing pro is. "Top of the mornin' to yer, sir" says the attendant.

Tiger nods a quick "hello" and bends forward to pick up the nozzle. As he does so, two tees fall out of his shirt pocket onto the ground.

"What are those?" asks the attendant.

"They're called tees" replies Tiger.

"Well, what on the god's earth are dey for?" inquires the Irishman.

"They're for resting my balls on when I'm driving", says Tiger.

"Fookin Jaysus", says the Irishman, "BMW thinks of everything!"

"Phil is brilliant, but he's nuts. There's something not quite right about that boy. Phil is watching a movie that only Phil can see. His mother told me, 'Phil was so clumsy as a little boy, we had to put a football helmet on him until he was 4 because he kept bumping into things.' I told her, 'Mary, Mary, I'm a writer, you can't keep handing me material like this.' So the next time I saw Phil I said, 'You didn't really wear a football helmet in the house until you were 4, did you?" He said, 'It was more like 5.'"

-David Feherty on Phil Mickleson

Jason Duffner was driving to his hotel after completing a practice round and noticed in his rear view Tiger Woods was following him. Not in the mood to talk, Duffner floored it. But the faster he drove, the closer Tiger would follow which went on and on until their speeds exceeded 100 mph.

Duffner turned down narrow alleyways at high speeds, braked his car into 180 degree spins and even drove his car down a flight of 30 building steps trying to lose Tiger.

Exhausted, Duffner pulled over and Tiger walked up to his car and said, "What the hell's wrong with you? I just wanted to talk?"

"Shit, after you took Amanda away, I thought you were following me to try and give her back to me."

"She could be adopted by Britney Spears and be better off. I want my sixteen year old daughter to have an enormous phone bill, a case of the giggles and be pissed off at me for killing her first three boyfriends. I don't want her out on the tour under that kind of pressure."

-David Feherty on life advice given to Michele Wie to join the tour.

The Pope and Tiger Woods died on the same day and because of an administrative mix up the Pope went to hell and Tiger Woods went to heaven.

The Pope tried to explain the situation to the administrative clerk in hell, and after checking the paperwork, the hell clerk admits that there was an error.

"However", the clerk explains, "it will be 24 hours before it can be rectified".

The next day the Pope is called up from the fires and Hell's staff bids him farewell. On the way up, the Pope meets Tiger Woods coming down from heaven and they stop to have a chat.

"Sorry about the mix up", apologizes the Pope.

"No problem" replied Tiger Woods.

Pope: "I am really anxious to get to heaven."

Tiger: "Why is that?"

Pope: "All my life I have wanted to meet the Virgin Mary."

Tiger: "You're a day late."

"Golf is like chasing a quinine pill around a cow pasture."

-Winston Churchill

The Pope met with the College of Cardinals to discuss a proposal from Shimon Peres, the former leader of Israel.

"Your holiness," said one of the Cardinals, "Mr. Peres wants to determine whether Jews or Catholics are superior, by challenging you to a golf match."

The Pope was greatly disturbed, as he had never held a golf club in his life.

"Not to worry," said the Cardinal, "we'll call America and talk to Jack Nicklaus. We'll make him a Cardinal; he can play Shimon Peres... We can't lose!"

Everyone agreed it was a good idea. The call was made and, of course, Jack was honored and agreed to play. The day after the match, Nicklaus reported to the Vatican to inform the Pope of his success in the match. "I came in second, your Holiness," said Nicklaus.

"Second?!!" exclaimed the surprised Pope.
"You came in second to Shimon Peres?!!"

"No," said Nicklaus, "second to Rabbi Spieth."

"I have to drink it slowly and not out of a can. I need some ice. I use to have 26-28 cans a day. Now I have 10-12 at most."

-John Daly

John Daly gave up golf for awhile and decided to try (among all things) Steeplehorse racing.

"Well John, since you're new, we're going to start you out on "Feedbag". She's really fast and can jump like hell but before you reach a jump, you got to yell out, 'ally ooop' real loud.

"No problem," John replied. As he approached the first jump, John being a little embarrassed, didn't say anything and Feedbag crashed right through the rails of the jump breaking it all apart. Through the flying wood, Feedbag kept going and John was still on her headed straight for the second jump. This time John whispered in her ear, "ally ooop," but Feedbag crashed right through the second jump headed for the third jump. This time John yelled as loud as he could, "ALLY OOOP" and Feedbag took off like a rocket and cleared it easily.

John trotted back to the trainer. "What the hell's wrong with this horse? Is it stupid?"

"No, she ain't stupid, she's just blind."

2. JOKES FOR THE CLUBHOUSE BAR

A big game hunter just finished his golf round at a wilderness golf course near Banff, Alberta and walked into the clubhouse bar and after a bad round he was feeling depressed so he boasted to everyone at the bar about his hunting skills.

"I'm not a golfer but a great hunter," he said.

No one could dispute it, he was a marksman. He bragged on and on – anyone could blindfold him and he would recognize any animal's skin from its feel, and if he found the bullet hole he would even tell them the caliber the fatal bullet.

People started to glance away from his bragging, and then the hunter said, "I'll prove it! If I guess your question right, you buy a round of drinks and if I lose I'll buy a round of drinks."

So the bet was on. He was blindfolded carefully and one of the golfers took him to his first animal skin. After feeling it for a few moments, he announced "Bear." Then he felt the bullet hole and declared, "Shot with a .308 rifle." He was right.

They brought him another skin, one that someone had in their car trunk. He took a bit longer this time and then said, "Elk, Shot with a 7mm Mag rifle. He was right again.

Through the night, he proved his skills again and again, every time against a round of drinks. Finally he staggered up to his hotel room, drunk out of his mind, and went to sleep. His wife was already asleep when he arrived.

The next morning he got up and saw in the mirror that he had one hell of a shiner. He said to his wife, "I know I was drunk last night, but not drunk enough to get in a fight and not remember it. Where did I get this black eye?"

His wife angrily replied, "I gave it to you. You got into bed and put your hand down my panties. Then you fiddled around a bit and loudly announced, "Skunk, killed with an axe."

"These greens are so fast I have to hold my putter over the ball and hit it with the shadow."

-Sam Snead, on Augusta National

Jack and his wife Jane were celebrating their 40th wedding anniversary and the golf clubhouse dining room.

"Jane after all these years, I was wondering if you ever were unfaithful to me."

"Oh, Jack, I don't want to talk about..."

"Jane, I really want to know."

"Oh, alright. Three times."

"Three? Okay, when were they," asked Jack?

"Well Jack, remember when we first got married you really needed a loan to start your business and no bank would touch you? Well, remember the chief bank loan officer came over to the house with a check for you and had you sign all the loan papers?"

"Oh, Jane, you did that for me? I think even more of you now...but when was the second time?"

Remember when you had your heart attack and were close to death? No one wanted to operate on you. Then the best cardiac surgeon in town suddenly appeared and operated on you?"

"Oh, gosh Jane, I love you so much. You saved my life. So, when was the third time?"

"Well, Jack, remember last year when you wanted to be golf club captain and you were 27 votes short?"

"There's a force in the universe that makes things happen. And all you have to do is to get in touch with it, stop thinking, and let things happen, and be the ball."

-Chevy Chase, Caddyshack

A true story:

Recently a routine police patrol parked outside a bar at a golf course in Texas. Shortly before closing, the officer sees a man carrying golf clubs leaving so intoxicated that he could barely walk. The man stumbled and bumbled around the parking lot. The officer remained quiet observing him. The man again stumbled for what seemed an eternity trying his keys in five different vehicles.

Finally, he found his pickup truck and tried to throw his clubs in the back but fell down trying and his golf bag and clubs fell out and tumbled on top of him. He sat there looking at this clubs and bag for a few minutes as a number of other patrons left the bar and drove off.

Finally, he gathered everything up, got into his truck, started the engine, and switched the wipers on and off, even though it was a clear moonlit summer night. Then he flicked the blinkers on and off a couple of times, honked the horn and switched on the lights. He moved the vehicle forward a few inches, reversed a little and then remained still for a few more minutes as some more of the other patrons' vehicles left.

Finally, when his was the only vehicle left in the parking lot, he pulled out and drove slowly down the road. The police officer, having waited patiently all this time, now started up his patrol car, and put on his emergency lights and pulled the man over.

"Good evening, officer," the golfer said.

"License and registration please?" Have you been drinking tonight?" said the officer.

"No, sir, not a drop."

The officer administered a breathalyzer test. To his amazement, the breathalyzer indicated no evidence that the man had consumed any alcohol at all!

Dumbfounded, the officer said, "I'll have to ask you to accompany me to the police station. This breathalyzer equipment must be broken."

"I seriously doubt it', said the truly proud golfer. Tonight I'm the designated decoy."

A mother in law said to her daughter in law who had just given birth, "I don't mean to be rude but he doesn't look anything like my son."

The daughter-in-law lifted her hospital gown and said, "I don't mean to be rude either, but this is a pussy, not a fucking photo-copier."

-unknown

Four golfers were sitting in the bar having a beer after a round. "My wife's got a lot of nerve being pissed at me," said Charlie.

You mean your wife won't let you out to play golf?" said another golfer teasing him.

"No, that's not it," explained Charlie. "I insist on making love in the dark, and after 20 years she turns on the light, and finds me holding a marital aid."

"What kind of a marital aid," said another golfer?

"A fuckin' vibrator! Okay? Well, she goes ballistic, and says, 'You impotent bastard! How could you lie to me all these years?'"

"Oh shit! You really impotent Charlie," asked another golfer?

"Yeah, so what?"

"Charlie, your wife should be pissed. Why didn't you tell her?" said another golfer.

"Oh she's got a lot of nerve alright. I looked her straight in the eye and calmly said, "I'll explain the toy, you explain the kids....."

"This is a hybrid. This is a cross, ah, of Bluegrass, Kentucky Bluegrass, Featherbed Bent, and Northern California Sensemilia. The amazing stuff about this is, that you can play 36 holes on it in the afternoon, take it home and just get stoned to the bejeezus belt that night on this stuff."

-Bill Murray, Caddyshack

A golfer finished his round and went to the clubhouse for a beer. He sits down and sees a huge ugly overweight guy talking to a very attractive woman. He thinks "yeah right."

Suddenly the girl slaps the huge man. The huge guy turns back to his beer laughing. After a little while he looks back -- and to his amazement, the girl and the huge guy are now really chummy and later they leave the bar together. The guy thinks what the fuck? . . .

A few days go by and the guy walks into the clubhouse after another round and the same scenario repeats itself -- with the huge fat guy, this time with a different girl -- the hottest in the bar and he watches the same thing unfold and the girl slaps the guy. The guy then says something, the girl melts and they leave the bar together. Now the golfer is totally confused.

A week later the same golfer again walks into the clubhouse bar after finishing a round and sees the huge ugly guy again sitting by himself. He walks up to the huge guy and says, "I see you in here hooking up with beautiful women and, well . . . you must have a very unusual method for doing it . . . what's your secret?

The huge guy says, "I really shouldn't tell you, it's a family secret."

"Please, I've got to know."

"Okay, since I'm leaving town tomorrow I'll tell you. What I do is tell her something extremely offensive like, 'tickle your pussy with a feather?' and the girl usually freaks out or slaps me. And then I say "whoa whoa, all I said was isn't it nice weather we're having. At which point she feels guilty for having slapped me. I use that guilt to get her in bed with me."

The guy replies, "and that works for you?"

"Yeah, every time, the guy replies. "Go try it yourself!"

So the golfer gets off the barstool and walks up to the hottest girl in the bar, taps her on the shoulder and she turns around. He says, "Slap your cunt with a nine iron?"

The woman looks astonished and says, WHAT DID YOU SAY??"

The guy replies, "I said it's fucking rainin' outside."

"Wait up, girls; I got a salami I gotta hide still."

-Bill Murray, Caddyshack

A Canadian guy, an American guy, a Japanese guy, and an Arab guy walk into the golf clubhouse bar after a round of golf. They all have a couple of beers, and get to bragging.

The American guy boasts, "I'm so lucky, I have 4 beautiful children, one more and I would have a basketball team. Wow!"

Not to be outdone, the Canadian guy says, "I'm luckier than you, I have 5 gifted children, one more and I could form a hockey team, eh?"

So, the Japanese guy chimes in with, "Well, I surely have both of you topped. I have 8 children. Just one more and I would have a baseball team, banzai!"

Pausing, briefly, the Arab guy replies, "Well, I am betting I have all you beat. My harem houses 17 wives, one more and I would have a golf course!

"Mistakes are part of the game. It's how well you recover from them, that's the mark of a great player."

-Alice Cooper

Four golfers went to Las Vegas on a golfing trip and after a losing most of their money at the blackjack tables; they decided to stay off the strip in a budget motel.

Standing at the registration desk, one of the golfers feeling very sorry for himself and feeling he's got nothing to lose guys complains to the owner, "Yeah, when the say what happens in Vegas stays in Vegas, they're really talking about our fuckin' money!" Then he spies a picture of the owner of the motel showing him with 18 daughters!

So he asks the owner, "Can I sleep with your 18 daughters?"

The owner says, "No, you can sleep with the pigs out back."

The second man asks the owner, "Can I sleep with your 18 daughters?"

The owner says, "No, you can sleep with the cows."

The third man asks the owner, "Can I sleep with your 18 daughters?"

The owner says, "No, you can sleep with the chickens."

The fourth man says, "Look, I don't want to sleep with your daughters, just give me a small room?"

The owner surprisingly says, "You can sleep with my 18 daughters."

In the morning the four men check out and the first man says "I slept like a pig."

The second man says, "I slept like a cow."

The third man says, "I slept like a chicken."

The fourth man said "I didn't sleep at all but dreamt I was a golfer playing 17 holes putting my stick in every one and I've got one more hole to play!"

The owner jumps up and kicks him swiftly in the groin. The man falls over in excruciating pain. The owner continues to stomp on the man's groin, shouting, "You dirty fucker! You won't be finishing your round since you're out of balls."

"The most important shot in golf is the next one."

-Ben Hogan

A very avid golfer toured Scotland playing little known golf courses in rural country areas. He found a course near Brecon Beacons in Wales. He loved the course so much; he later bought a little sheep farm nearby on a mountain.

He went about golfing and sheep ranching and loved it as much as he thought he would. But he was lonely, so one evening he bicycled 10 miles to the closest pub. It was a rustic little place on a rocky outcropping. The only other customers were two older men in a corner playing dominoes.

"Where are all the women?" the new farmer asked.

"You'll not find any women in these parts, I'm afraid! Not in many years!" replied one of the old men.
"So what do you do for, uh, companionship?"

"When the urge overwhelms you, you just grab a sheep and give it a good shagging! No shame in it -- we all have to do it."

The golfer said that was disgusting and he would never do it, drained his pint and went home. But a month later he was herding his sheep and felt so randy he couldn't take it anymore. He grabbed a sheep, got on his knees and starting humping it.

Suddenly, a peal of laughter broke out behind him. He spun his head around and saw the two old farmers, who were cutting across his field, pointing at him, laughing, and pounding their knees.

"You said that everyone around here shags sheep!" yelled the golfer as he pulled his pants back up.

"Yeah," replied one of the old men. "But we don't fuck the ugly ones!"

"A bad attitude is worse than a bad swing."

-Payne Stewart

Same golfer walks into a pub in Brecon Beacon and sits down next to an old man. They strike up a conversation and the old man says, "Laddie, do ya play the golf course?"

"As much as I can," he replied.

"I built that golf course with me own hands, but do they call me Evan Jones the course builder? No sir."

The golfer nods appreciatively and the old man says, "Do you ya see this pub here? I built this pub with me own hands, but do they call me Evan Jones the pub builder? No sir."

The guy nods again and finally the old man says, "Arrgh...but ya fuck one goat..."

"Golf is a puzzle without an answer. I've played the game for 50 years and I still haven't the slightest idea on how to play it."

-Gary Player

The Three Worst Chinese Torture Tests for The Disobedient Golfer:

An American golfer is out playing a very remote Chinese golf course near the Mongolian border way out in the mountain wilderness. The remote, rarely used course is vast with very rough terrain. The golfer becomes hopelessly lost searching for his golf ball. He wanders aimlessly for three weeks eating anything he could forage and he's been reduced to sleeping in caves and under trees.

One afternoon the golfer staggers up to an old home in the woods. It has vines covering most of it and there's nothing else around. he sees smoke coming out of the chimney.

He knocks on the door and a very small and very old Chinese man answers, with a gray beard almost down to the ground. The old man says, "What do you want?"

The golfer says "I've been wandering for the past three weeks and haven't had a decent meal or sleep since that time. Kind sir, I would be most gracious if I could have a meal and sleep in your house for tonight"

The old man says "I'll let you come in on one condition: You cannot touch my granddaughter."

The golfer, exhausted and hungry readily agrees, saying "I promise, I promise, I won't cause you any trouble. Can you show me how to get back to the golf course and I'll be on my way tomorrow morning."

The old man squints at him and says, "Okay, but if I catch you then I'll give you the three worst Chinese torture tests ever known to man."

"Okay, Okay," said the weary golfer and staggers into the house thinking to himself, what kind of woman would live out in the wilderness all her life?

Well, that night, the golfer comes down to eat after a hot bath, and meets the beautiful granddaughter. She was the most beautiful

Chinese woman he had ever seen. Before he'd been lost for three weeks, he had many months without companionship. And the young woman was eager for a young man and they both couldn't keep their eyes off each other.

That night, the man snuck into the woman's bedroom and they had a great time, but kept the noise down to a minimum. The man crept back to his room later that night thinking to himself, "Any three torture tests would be worth it after that."

Well, the next morning the man awoke to a heavy weight on his chest. He opened his eyes and there was this huge rock on his chest. On the rock was a small sign saying "1st Chinese torture test: 50 lb rock on your chest".

"What a lame torture test," the man thought to himself and he got up and walked over to the window. He opened the shutter and threw the rock out. On the backside of the rock is another sign saying "2nd worst Chinese torture test: Rock tied to right testicle".

The man, seeing the rock was too far out the window to be retrieved, jumped out the window after the rock. Outside the window is a third sign saying "3rd worst Chinese torture test: Left testicle tied to bedpost".

"Those years on the golf course as a caddie, boy, those people were something. They were vulgar, some were alcoholics, racist, and they were very difficult people to deal with. A lot of them didn't have a sense of humor."

-Martin Sheen

A bus full of Nuns falls off a cliff and they all die instantly and arrive at the gates of heaven and meet St. Peter. St. Peter says to them "Sisters, welcome to heaven. In a moment I will let you all though the pearly gates, but before I do that; I must ask each of you a single question. Please form a single-file line."

So they line up in single-file. St. Peter turns to the first Nun in the line and asks her "Sister, have you ever touched a penis?"

The Sister Responds "Well... there was this one time... that I kinda sorta... touched one with the tip of my pinky finger..."

St. Peter says "Alright Sister, now dip the tip of your pinky finger in the Holy Water, and you may be admitted." and she did so.

St. Peter then turned to the second nun in line and said, "Sister, have you ever touched a penis?"

"Well.... There was this one time... that I held one for a moment..."

"Alright Sister, now just wash your hands in the holy water, and you may be admitted" and she does so.

St. Peter then hears a noise - a jostling in the line. It seems that one nun is trying to cut in front of another! St. Peter sees this and asks the nun "Sister Susan, what are you doing? There is no rush!"

Sister Susan responds "Well if I'm going to have to gargle this stuff, I'd rather do it before Sister Mary sticks her ass in it!"

"I learned one thing from jumping motorcycles that was of great value on the golf course, the putting green especially: Whatever you do, don't come up short."

-Evil Knievel

A golfer walks into the clubhouse restaurant after a round and sees a new sign hanging over the bar that reads: CHEESEBURGER: $4.50 CHICKEN SANDWICH: $6.50 HAND JOB: $20.00 He walks up to the bar and beckons one of the three exceptionally attractive blonde waitresses.

"Can I help you," she asks?"

"I was wondering," whispers the golfer. "Are you the one who gives the hand jobs?"

"Yes," she purrs. "I am."

The golfer replies, "Well, wash your hands. I want a cheeseburger."

A "gimmie" can best be defined as an agreement between two golfers ... Neither of whom can putt very well.

-Anonymous

Several golfers are in the locker room getting ready to play when a mobile phone on a bench rings. One of the guys picks it up and answers it. Everyone else in the locker room stops to listen.

Golfer: Hello?

Woman: Hi Honey, it's me are you at the club?

Golfer: Yes.

Woman: I'm at the mall and found this beautiful coat. It's only $900. Okay if I buy it?

Golfer: Sure, go ahead if you really like it.

Woman: I stopped at the Jaguar dealership and they've got a brand new F-Type in and I really like it.

Golfer: How much is it?

Woman: $70,000.

Golfer: Well okay buy it but make sure you get all the options.

Woman: Fantastic! Oh, one more thing. The house we saw last year is back on the market and the dropped the price to $1.1 million.

Golfer: Well go ahead and offer $1,050,000 and see if they take it. If not give them full price.

Woman: That's great! Will do. I love you honey. You are so good to me!

Golfer: Well you're worth every penny. Love you too. Bye.

The golfer hangs up. The other guys in the locker room are speechless and staring at him with their mouths open.

The golfer looks at them and says, "Anybody know whose phone this is?"

"Older women are best, because they always think they may be doing it for the last time."

-Ian Fleming

A very good young golfer playing in a local tournament was being followed around the course by an older woman totally enamored with him. She just couldn't take her eyes off him. She waited around until after the round and went up and told him how much she admired him and his play and his shooting a 69 that day. She offered to take him home for dinner which he accepted.

"A 69! It was great to watch such a handsome man like you play and you're only 21 years old! You've got a great career in front of you," she said over dinner.

"Yeah, I don't shoot a 69 very often on that course," he politely replied.

The enamored woman gave him a wink and said, "How about you and I do a 69?"

The young man a bit inexperienced asked, "What's a 69?"

"Well, you put your head between my legs, and I put my head between your legs."

The young man accepted and they took off their clothes but just as he put his head between her legs, she let out a roaring fart. "Oh! I'm so sorry, please excuuuse me," she laughed.

The young man nodded then put tried to put his head between her legs and again she lets out another roaring fart right in his face. "Oh! Sorry again," she said.

The young man got up and got dressed and walked out saying, "I'm not doing that another 67 times."

3. OLDER GOLFER JOKES

Two very old retired lawyers went golfing and both sliced their drives. They were deep in the rough searching for their errant tee shots. Neither of them wanted to lose a new ball so they searched and searched and eventually wandered off the golf course and came upon a pair of tracks. They stopped and examined the tracks closely. The first old lawyer announced, "My ball hit these tracks and probably rolled down this way somewhere and I'm going to follow these tracks.

The second old lawyer responded, "Our golf balls couldn't possibly go that way down these tracks – at least not very far and I'm not going to waste my round searching for your fucking ball in that direction. Besides any idiot could easily see by looking at the level of the land our balls probably went the opposite way!"

Each old attorney believed himself to have the superior analysis of the situation and they both bitterly argued on and on. Neither of them would back off from their argument. They were still arguing when the train hit them.

"I don't feel old. I don't feel anything till noon. That's when it's time for my nap."

-Bob Hope

A retired policeman was sick of playing golf at his club. Four times a week is enough. When he wasn't playing golf, his wife nagged him too much. I wish I could get back doing something worthwhile, he thought. He had heard from police brothers that the FBI had an open position for an asset (an assassin).

After all the background checks, interviews and testing were completed, the policeman made the final field of 3 possible candidates. For the final test, the FBI agents took one of the men to a large metal door and handed him a gun."We must know that you will follow your instructions no matter what the circumstances. Inside the room you will find your wife sitting in a chair... we need you to kill her," the man said.

"You can't be serious. I could never shoot my wife."

The agent said, "Then you're not the right man for this job. Take your wife and go home."

The second man was given the same instructions. He took the gun and went into the room. All was quiet for about 5 minutes.

The man came out with tears in his eyes, "I tried, but I can't kill my wife."

The agent said, "You don't have what it takes. Take your wife and go home."

Finally, the retired policeman was last man left and was given the same instructions, to kill his wife. He took the gun and went into the room. Shots were heard, one after another. They heard screaming, crashing, banging on the walls. After a few minutes, all was quiet. The door opened slowly and there stood the man, wiping the sweat from his brow. "Some idiot loaded the gun with blanks," he said. "I had to strangle that bitch to death".

"In the Bob Hope Golf Classic, the participation of President Gerald Ford was more than enough to remind you that the nuclear button was at one stage at the disposal of a man who might have either pressed it by mistake or else pressed it deliberately to obtain room service."

-Clive James

An elderly lady was concerned about her husband's hearing. It seemed that every time she would call him, he wouldn't respond. So, the lady went to the doctor to ask his advice. The doctor said to her, "You play golf with him. Stand a distance away from him and tell him something - ask his advice on how to play a shot. Continue to move closer to him until he responds to your question so you know exactly how far away he is from you when he finally hears you."

She thought this was a great idea. The next time they were out on the course, she asked from a distance "Herbert what club should I play for this shot?"

There was no response. She moved 10 feet closer. Again she yelled, "Herbert, what club should I play?"

Still no response, so she moved another 15 feet closer to where she was now practically face to face with her husband. She yelled even louder this time, "HERBERT, what club should I play for this shot?"

Herbert yelled back at her, "For the THIRD time, use a 5 iron!"

"Follow through: The part of the swing that takes place before the ball has been hit, but before the club has been thrown."

-Bob Hope

An old man and his wife are out playing golf and run into a back up at a par 3 with two foursomes ahead of them waiting in their carts to tee off.

After sitting there a few minutes the old man farts and says, "Seven Points."

His wife slowly turns to him and says, "What in the world was that?"

The old man replied, "It's fart football! Might as well play with this delay."

A few minutes later the wife lets one go and says - "Touchdown, tie score!"

After about five minutes the old man farts again and says - "Touchdown, I'm ahead 14 to 7!"

Not to be out done the wife rips another one and says, - "Touchdown, tie score!"

Five seconds go by and she lets out a squeaker and says - "Field goal, I lead 17 to 14!"

Now the pressures on and the old man refuses to get beaten by a woman so he strains real hard but to no avail. Realizing a defeat is totally unacceptable he gives it everything he has and shits his shorts and the shit leaks all over his seat.

The wife looks and says, "What the heck was that?"

The old man replied, "Half-time, Switch sides!"

"To find a man's true character, play golf with him."

P.G. Wodehouse

An elderly couple from Florida went on vacation in Texas, and just finished a round of golf. While the man was waiting for his wife to join him for a drink he spied a pair of authentic cowboy boots which he always wanted from the time he was a small boy and bought them but hid them from his wife wanting to surprise her later.

When they got back to Florida, he put on the boots and walks into the living room where his wife is reading a magazine and announces, "Notice anything different about me?"

The wife looks up, gives him the once over and then says, "Nope."

Frustrated he storms off to the bathroom, takes off all of his clothes and steps out wearing only the boots and says, "Notice anything different now?"

She sighs, closes her magazine, and says, "It's hanging down, it was hanging down yesterday, and it'll hang down again tomorrow."

Now furious as hell, he shouts, "Do you know why it's hanging down? It's hanging down because it's looking at my new boots!"

She replies, "Shoulda bought a hat. Ya shoulda bought a hat."

"I guess there is nothing that will get your mind off everything like golf. I have never been depressed enough to take up the game, but they say you get so sore at yourself you forget to hate your enemies."

-Will Rogers

An old man strolled by a golf course and noticed a youngster playing golf with his dog riding alongside in the golf cart. The youngster would stop, hit his ball then drive up to the next ball and the dog would get out, jump up and take a club out of the golf bag with his teeth and hit the ball down the fairway. The old man continued to watch in astonishment for a while. He went up to them and exclaimed, "I can hardly believe my eyes! That's the smartest dog I've ever seen."

"Nah, he's not so smart," the youngster replied. "I've beaten him three games out of five.

"There's a perfect shot out there tryin' to find each and every one of us.... All we got to do is get ourselves out of its way, to let it choose us.... Can't see that flag as some dragon you got to slay.... You got to look with soft eyes.... See the place where the tides and the seasons and the turnin' of the Earthy, all come together...where everything that is, becomes one.... You got to seek that place with your soul."

-Legend of Bagger Vance

A schoolteacher was taking her first golfing lesson. "Is the word spelt p-u-t or p-u-t-t?" she asked the instructor.

"P-u-t-t is correct," he replied. "P-u-t means to place a thing where you want it."

"Yes, we all know that," replied the schoolteacher.

The instructor smiled and said, "P-u-t-t means merely a vain attempt to do the same thing."

"I can't wait to be that age and hanging out with a bunch of people hanging out all day playing golf and going to the beach, all my own age. We'd be laughing and having a good time and getting loopy on our prescription drugs and driving golf carts around. I can't wait."

-Cameron Diaz

Two old golfers, Arnie and Jack, sit on a park bench feeding pigeons and talking about golf. Arnie turns to Jack and asks, "Do you think there's golf in Heaven?"

Jack thinks about it for a minute and replies, "I don't really know. But let's make a pact -- if I die first, I'll come back and tell you if there's golf in Heaven, and if you die first, you'll do the same." They shake on it and sadly, a few months later, poor Arnie passes on. Soon afterward, Jack's in the park feeding the pigeons by himself and hears a voice whisper, "Jack... Jack...."

Jack responds, "Arnie! Is that you?"

"Yes it is, Jack," whispers Arnie's ghost.

Jack, still amazed, asks, "So, is there golf in Heaven?"

"Well," says Arnie, "I've got good news and bad news."

"Give me the good news first," says Jack. Arnie says, "Well, there is golf in Heaven."

Jack says, "That's great! What news could be bad enough to ruin that?"

Arnie sighs and whispers, "We've got a tee time on Friday."

"What most people don't understand is that UFOs are on a cosmic tourist route. That's why they're always seen in Arizona, Scotland, and New Mexico. Another thing to consider is that all three of those destinations are good places to play golf. So there's possibly some connection between aliens and golf."

-Alice Cooper

An elderly couple played the golf course twice a week primarily for exercise since they had trouble keeping track of their shots. They had trundlers with numbered dials to turn and keep a count of their shots but would forget to use the counters as well.

After golf they went home and decided to visit their doctor about their memory lapses. Their doctor tells them that many people find it useful to write themselves little notes.

When they get home, the wife says, "Dear, will you please go to the kitchen and get me a dish of ice cream? And maybe write that down so you won't forget?"

"Nonsense," says the husband, "I can remember a dish of ice cream."

"Well," says the wife, "I'd also like some strawberries and whipped cream on it."

"My memory's not all that bad," says the husband. "No problem -- a dish of ice cream with strawberries and whipped cream. I don't need to write it down." He goes to the kitchen; his wife hears pots and pans banging around. The husband finally emerges from the kitchen and presents his wife with a plate of bacon and eggs.

She looks at the plate and asks, "Hey, where's the toast I asked for?"

"For a competitive junkie like me, golf is a great solution because it smacks you in the face every time you think you have accomplished something. That to me has taken over a lot of the energy and competitiveness for basketball."

- Michael Jordan

An old guy in his Volvo is driving home from after playing a terrible round of golf when his wife calls him in his car. He answers using the car speaker.

"Honey", she says in a worried voice, "be careful. There was a bit on the news just now, some lunatic is driving the wrong way down the freeway".

"It's worse than that", he replies, "There are hundreds of them!"

"A shot that goes into the cup is pure luck. But a shot that goes within two feet of the hole is skill."

-Ben Hogan

Dear Dr Phil:

I came home from golf and decided to take a nap and found myself watching my next door neighbor's wife sunbathing topless from my bedroom window.

As I was jerking off, I turned to notice my wife was just standing there, arms folded...watching me.

Is she perverted or what?

"We learn so many things from golf, like how to suffer for instance."

-Bruce Lansky

Three men, a philosopher, a mathematician and a golfer, were out riding in a car when it crashed into a tree. The next thing they knew, they found themselves standing before the pearly gates of Heaven, where St. Peter and the Devil greeted all three of them.

"Gentlemen," the Devil started, "Due to the fact that Heaven is now overcrowded, St. Peter has agreed to limit the number of people entering Heaven. If anyone of you can ask me a question which I don't know or cannot answer, then you're worthy enough to go to Heaven; if not, then you'll come with me to Hell."

The philosopher then stepped up, "Okay, give me the most comprehensive report on Socrates' teachings."

With a snap of his finger, a stack of paper appeared next to the Devil. The philosopher read it and concluded it was correct.

"Then, go to Hell!" The Devil snapped his fingers again and the philosopher disappeared.

The mathematician stepped up and said, "Okay, tell me what number or concept equals infinity divided by infinity?

The Devil smiled and said, "That's easy, it equals the time you'll spend in hell." The Devil snapped his fingers and the mathematician disappeared.

The golfer then stepped forward and said, "Bring me a chair!" The Devil brought forward a chair. "Drill 7 holes on the seat." The Devil did just that. The golfer then sat on the chair and let out a very loud fart. Standing up, he asked, "Which hole did my fart come out from?"

The Devil inspected the seat and said, "The third hole from the right."

"Wrong," said the golfer, "It came out of my asshole, you asshole!"

The Devil shit his pants.

St. Peter opened the gates for the golfer.

"Golf is the most fun you can have without taking your clothes off."

-Chi Chi Rodriguez

A woman golfer having many wrinkles from numerous hours in the sun playing golf decided to have a face lift for her birthday. She spent $5000 and felt really good about the results.

Three weeks went by for healing and on her way home from her last doctor's visit she stopped at a dress shop to look around. As she was leaving, she said to the sales clerk, "I hope you don't mind me asking, but how old do you think I am?"

"About 35,"she replied.

"I'm actually 47," the woman said, feeling really happy.

After that she went into the pro shop to buy new younger looking golf wear and asked the shop cashier the same question.

He replied, "Oh, you look about 29."

"I am actually 47!" she said, feeling really good. She left but as she was getting into her car she saw an old man just behind her and asked the old man the same question.

He replied, "I am 85 years old and my eyesight is going. But when I was young there was a sure way of telling a woman's age. If I put my hand up your skirt I will be able to tell your exact age."

There was no one around, so the woman said, "What the hell?" and sat in her car and let him slip his hand up her skirt. The old geezer grinned and slipped his hand under her skirt and smoothly rubbed and rubbed. She was getting hot and bothered and almost came when the geezer slipped his hand out and said, "OK, You are 47."

Stunned, the woman said, "That was brilliant! How did you do that?"

The old man replied, "I was behind you in line at the pro shop."

"The fun you get from golf is in direct ratio to the effort you don't put into it."

-Bob Allen

Two guys are putting on a green right next to a cemetery. After one guy putts, he notices the other guy is standing on the green, head bowed, with his hat off. In the distance there's a hearse followed by a funeral procession of cars passing them on the way to the cemetery. The other guy is still standing there somber with his hat over his heart.

When the funeral procession completely passed them, he asks, "Why did you put your hat over your heart?"

The other guy replied, "Well hell, we were married for almost 40 years. It's the least I could do."

"A woman in labor is in tremendous pain and screaming profanity after profanity at her husband from her hospital bed. "You did this to me you fucking bastard!" Husband says, "Hey, don't blame me! I wanted to stick it in your ass, but N-O-O-O-O, you said that might hurt!"

-Anonymous

An old lady in a nursing home is driving her golf cart up and down the sidewalks making sounds like she's driving a race car. As she's turning the corner, an old man jumps out and says, "Excuse me ma'am but you were speeding. Can I see your driver's license?"

She digs around in her purse a little, pulls out a candy wrapper, and hands it to him. He looks it over, gives her a warning and sends her on her way.

Up and down the walkways she goes again. Again, the same old man jumps out and says, "Excuse me ma'am but I saw you cross over the center line back there. Can I see your registration please?"

She digs around in her purse a little, pulls out a store receipt and hands it to him. He looks it over, gives her another warning and sends her on her way.

She zooms off again up and down the walkways weaving all over. As she turns the same corner, the old man is stark naked and has an erection!

The old lady looks at his dick and says, "Oh no- not the Breathalyzer again!"

"A lot of guys who have never choked have never been in a position to do so."

-Tom Watson

An old man in an assisted living facility tells the head nurse, "My dick just died."

"Oh we're so sorry to hear that, Mr. Johnson. May your penis rest in peace.

Yes, me and my dick had lots of fun together. It was the best club in my golf bag! Haha!

The next day, Mr. Johnson is walking the halls with his penis hanging out of his pajamas. The nurse comes up to him and says, "Mr. Johnson, you told us your penis had died?"

"Today is the viewing."

"It would be easier to pick a broken nose than a winner in that group."

-David Feherty

One Christmas the family came home to celebrate. All four kids in the family were successful and had become wealthy doctors and lawyers. Over the break they were eating out and talking about what great gifts they had given their old mother, living in a far away city, for Christmas.

The first brother says: "I have built a big new house for mum with its own private 9 hole golf course."

The second brother says:"I spent one hundred thousand dollars to have a cinema built in her new house. "

The third says: "I ordered my regular Mercedes dealer to deliver a luxurious convertible to her "

The fourth brother says: "Well, Mom loves to read the Bible and you know how bad her eyesight has become. I recently came across a priest, who told me about a parrot that can recite the entire Bible. It took twenty priests well over 12 years to teach him all that but nowadays that parrot's so good that you only need to say the chapter and the verse and he recites it. I had to promise to give one hundred thousand dollars to the Church every year for the next twenty years, but well, mum is worth every penny.

Christmas is over and mum sends her boys a thank you note: On the first she writes "John, the house that you have built for me, is so big that I use just one room, although I have to clean the whole house. The golf course is great, you know how I love to play the game but I'm having trouble seeing where to hit the ball. Nevertheless, many thanks! "

The second was told: "Charley, that cinema has got Dolby surround and 50 people fit in easily. Wonderful! But all my friends and acquaintances are dead, I'm deaf and almost blind, so I never go in there. But thanks for the good idea! "

On the third: "Pete, I'm too old to go on a trip and my groceries are delivered at home so the Mercedes is rusting outside. But it was a nice idea. Many thanks! "

And the fourth: "My dear Hank, you're the only

son who thinks and cares enough about me to think of something that I really enjoy! The chicken was delicious! Thank you very much!

"I have to admit, I sometimes wonder how much more successful I would have been as a coach had it not been for my spending summers on the golf course. I could have watched more film, that's for sure. One advantage Joe Paterno had over me was that he didn't play golf."

-Lou Holtz

Two ninety year old golfers teed off the first hole on their usual weekly game. One said to the other, "Ah it's great to be alive. I've never felt better... I have an 18-year old bride who is pregnant with my child. What do you think of that?"

The other golfer replied, "My grandson and his friends took me out hunting and I was in a hurry and picked up my umbrella instead of my rifle by mistake. When I got to the creek, I saw a beaver. I raised his umbrella and went "bang, bang, bang", and the beaver fell dead. What do you think of that?"

The other 90-year old with the 18 year old bride replied, "I'd say somebody else shot the beaver."

The other said, "My point exactly".

"There is etiquette in golf, but it's not any harder to learn than what to do at a dinner party. Actually, it's probably easier. And these days, there are a lot more women out there than there used to be. It's not like when I was young. I was always the only girl on the range."

-Paula Creamer, LPGA

An old retired golfer gave some good advice:

"It is important for men to remember that, as women grow older it becomes harder for them to maintain the same quality of housekeeping as they did when they were younger. When you notice this, try not to yell at them. Some are oversensitive and there is nothing worse than an oversensitive woman.

"Let me relate how I handled the situation with my wife Matilda:

"When I retired a few years ago, it became necessary for her to get a full-time job along with her part-time job, both for the extra income and for the health benefits we needed. Shortly after she started working I noticed she was beginning to show her age. I usually get home from the Golf Club about the same time she gets home from work. Although she knows how hungry I am, she almost always says she has to rest for half an hour or so before she starts dinner. Instead I tell her to take her time and to wake me when she puts the dinner on the table. I generally have lunch at the Café at the Club so eating out is not reasonable. I'm ready for a home cooked dinner when I come home.

"She used to do the dishes as soon as we finished eating, but now it's usual for the dishes to sit on the table for several hours after dinner. I do what I can diplomatically, by reminding her several times each evening that 'The dishes won't clean themselves.' I know she really appreciates this as it does seem to motivate her to get them done before she goes to bed.

"Another symptom of aging is complaining. For example, she will say it is difficult for her to find the time to pay the monthly bills during her lunch hour. But boys, we take them for better or worse, so I just smile and offer her encouragement. I tell her to stretch it out over two or even three days. That way she wouldn't have to rush so much. I remind her that missing her lunch completely now and then won't hurt her, if you know what I mean.

"I like to think that tact is one of my strong points. When doing simple jobs she seems to think she needs more rest periods. She had to take a break when she was only half finished mowing the backyard. I try not to make a scene. I am a fair man. I tell her to fix herself a nice big cold glass of freshly squeezed Lemonade and just sit for a while. And, as long as she's making one for herself, she may as well make one for me too. I know that I probably look like a Saint in the way that I support Denise. I'm not saying that showing this much consideration is easy. Some will find it impossible!

"Nobody knows better than I do how frustrating women get when they get older. However guys, even if you use just a little more tact and less criticism of your aging wife because of this article, I will consider writing it, was well worthwhile. After all, we were put on this earth to help each other."

A week later, the narrator of this story died suddenly of a perforated rectum. He had a 48 inch Driver jammed up his ass head first with only a few inches of the grip sticking out of his asshole. There was a sledge hammer found next to him. His wife, Matilda, was arrested and charged with murder but the all women jury took only 10 minutes to find her not guilty, accepting her defense her husband, somehow without looking, accidently sat down on his own golf club.

4. BLONDE GOLFER JOKES

Two croupiers are sitting at a crap table at a Vegas casino. The casino is extremely busy due to a professional golf tournament that weekend. But no players were playing at the crap table.

Suddenly, a very attractive blonde woman enters and bets $20,000 on a roll, saying: "I hope you don't mind, but I feel very lucky when I play naked."

With that, she unbuttons, takes her dress and underwear off, then throws her clothes wildly in the air. Her huge tits blast out - bouncing up and down, up and down. She grabs the dice and yells: "Come on baby, mama needs new clothes!"

She looks with agony at the rolling dice and as soon as the dice stop rolling, she starts wildly jumping up and down, then jumps on one of the croupiers and wraps her long beautiful legs around him screaming: "YES, YES, YES I WON!" She then shoves her tits in the other croupier's face and embraces him, taking a huge stack of her winnings. She picks up her clothes and disappears.

The croupiers look dumbfounded at each other. Eventually, one asks: "Did you see what she rolled?"

"I don't know, I thought you were watching!"

"It's great to be blonde. With low expectations it's great to surprise people."

-Pamela Anderson

While all that was happening with the naked blonde at the crowded casino full of golfers and golf fans, at the crap table in the previous joke, another blonde is at a soda machine wearing a Ricky Fowler hat.

She puts in a dollar and gets a soda. She does this again and again. A man in line behind her asks why she's taking so long.

She says, "Can't you see I'm winning?"

"In one moment you're bleeding. The next minute you're hemorrhaging. The next minute you're painting the Mona Lisa."

-Mac O'Grady

A Blonde was out golfing with her brunette friend. The brunette tells her she's out of tees and asked the blonde if she had any. The blonde golfer said no so the brunette tells the blonde to stoop down and hold the ball just off the ground using the tips of her fingers. It was a bit awkward but the brunette managed to hit some great drives.

After the round, the blonde left early and went to the doctor. She walked in and said, "Doctor, what's the problem with me? When I touch my arm, ouch! It hurts... When I touch my leg, ouch! It hurts... When I touch my head, ouch! It hurts... When I touch my chest, ouch! It really hurts!"

The Doctor replies: "Your fingers are broken."

"I'm not offended by all the dumb blonde jokes because I know I'm not dumb … and I also know that I'm not blonde."

-Dolly Parton

A young ventriloquist is touring the clubs and one night he's doing a show in a small club in a small town in Arkansas. With his dummy on his knee, he's going through his usual dumb blonde jokes when a blonde woman in the fourth row stands on her chair and starts shouting:

"I've heard enough of your stupid blonde jokes. What makes you think you can stereotype women that way? Some of the best lady golfers in the world are blonde such as Suzann Petersen? Or, Natalie Gulbis? What does the color of a person's hair have to do with her worth as a human being? It's guys like you who keep women like me from being respected at work and in the community and from reaching our full potential as a person, because you and your kind continue to perpetuate discrimination against, not only blondes, but women in general...and all in the name of humor!"

The ventriloquist is embarrassed and begins to apologize, when the blonde yells, "You stay out of this, mister! I'm talking to that little idiot on your knee!"

"That ball is so far left, Lassie couldn't find it if it was wrapped in bacon."

-David Feherty

A blonde, a brunette, and a redhead are out golfing and come across an enchanted bridge and as they step onto the bridge, the golf course suddenly becomes a Magical Fairyland. They continue across the bridge and run into a beautiful fairy.

The fairy says that they can be granted a transformation if they jump off the bridge and call out their wish. So the brunette immediately jumps off the bridge and yells "Eagle!" She turns into a beautiful bird of prey and flies away.

The redhead jumps off the bridge and yells out "Salmon!" She turns into a gorgeous shimmering salmon and swims upstream to spawn.

The blonde is amazed and at this point very excited and awkwardly scrambles up the side of the bridge to the jump off point, twists her ankle and yells, "Shit" then falls of the bridge.

"The only way I'd be caught without make-up is if my radio fell in the bathtub while I was taking a bath and electrocuted me and I was in between make-up at home. I hope my husband would slap a little lipstick on me before he took me to the morgue."

-Dolly Parton

A blonde is driving home from the golf course after a round but she was going fast and got pulled over by a police car.

A blonde woman cop gets out and walks up to the car and says, "I think you were going too fast. May I see your driver's license?"

The blonde golfer lady grabs her purse and rummages around through golf tees, ball markers, old scorecards, and then asks, "Um, what does it look like?"

The blonde cop says, "It's a little square thing and it has your picture on it."

The other blonde rummages through her purse again and spots a little square compact mirror. She pulls it out and sure enough, right there in the middle is her face and she hands it to the police officer.

The blonde cop looks at it and immediately hands it back, and says, "Okay, you're free to go. I didn't know you were a cop."

"Wal-Mart? Do they make walls there?"

-Paris Hilton talking about the chain store

Two blondes were playing golf one sunny Saturday morning. The first of the twosome teed off and watched in horror as her ball headed directly toward a foursome of men playing the next hole.

The ball hit one of the men, and he immediately clasped his hands together over his groin area, fell to the ground and proceeded to roll around in evident agony.

The blonde rushed down to the man and immediately began to apologize. "Please allow me to help. I'm a physical therapist and I know I could relieve your pain if you'd allow me," she told him earnestly.

"Ummph, oooh, nooo, I'll be alright. I'll be fine in a few minutes," he replied breathlessly as he remained in the fetal position still clasping his hands together in his groin.

But the blonde persisted, and he finally allowed her to help him. She gently took his hands away and laid them to the side, she loosened his pants, and she put her hands inside. She began to massage him. She then asked him "How does that feel?"

He replied "It feels great, but my thumb still hurts like hell."

"How can you tell your girlfriend's horny? You stick your hand down her pants and it feels like your feeding a horse."

-Anonymous

A not so bright golfer got on a bus full of nuns. He was trying to be polite as he could but one nun was amazing to look at and he got a huge erection. So he went up to her and said, "I want to have sex with you right now."

"No," replied the nun. "I am a woman of the lord I will never sleep with you."

The golfer got depressed, and on his way off the bus the bus driver told him that the nun goes to the church to pray every night at midnight. All he had to do was get a god mask and tell her to fuck him.

At exactly midnight the golfer spotted the nun go into the church. He put on his god mask and said to the nun, "I am god. You must fuck me."

The nun replied, "Only in the ass though." The golfer agreed and they fucked for hours.

When they were done the golfer took off his mask and shouted "Ha ha! I'm the golfer."

The nun took off her mask and said "Ha ha! I'm the bus driver."

"The way I see it, if you want the rainbow, you got to put up with the rain."

-Dolly Parton

A golfer quit a small pro tour not having any success and just started a new job working at a porno shop and was determined to make money and be successful.

His boss rushes out from the back and tells him that he has to leave for a while, and asks if he can handle the store on his first day. The golfer is somewhat reluctant, but with the boss's positive comments he finally agrees.

A few minutes later a white woman walks in and asks, "How much for the white dildo?"

He answers, "$35."

She: "How much for the black one?"

He: "$35 for the black one, they are the same price."

She: "I think I'll take the black one. I've never had a black one before." She pays him, and off she goes.

A little bit later a black woman comes in and asks "How much for the black dildo?"

He: "$35."

She: "How much for the white one?"

He: "$35 for the white one also, they are the same price."

She: "Hmmm...I think I'll take the white one. I've never had a white one before..." She pays him, and off she goes.

About an hour later a blonde woman comes in and asks, "How much are your dildos?"

He: "$35 for the white, $35 for the black."

She: "Hmmmmm....how much is that plaid one on the shelf?"

He: "Well, that's a very special dildo...it'll cost you $350."

She thinks for a moment and answers, "I'll take the plaid one, I've never had a plaid one before...." She pays him, and off she goes.

Finally, the boss returns and asks, "How did you do while I was gone?"

"I think I did pretty well, I sold one white dildo, one black dildo, and I sold your thermos for $350!"

5. JOKES FOR GOLF ROUND DELAYS, TEE BACKUPS, SLOW PLAY

If you're ever late for a tee time, tell this tale seriously to your buddies when you arrive. Act seriously flustered and apologetic (you'll get a bigger laugh):

Okay, so I was speeding trying to get here on time when out of nowhere I see a slight black flash then felt a thud under my tires.

I stopped and pulled over to see what I'd hit. There lying on the ground was a dead black cat. I moved it off the road completely angry at myself and got back in my car.

As I drove off I hear a siren and see the flashing lights in my rearview.

"Fuck!" I'm thinking to myself, I was already late for golf, I just killed a cat, and now a police officer is going to read me the riot act. I pull over and he comes up to my window and asks me to step out. So I do this, thinking I take the ticket then be on my way to golf.

"What seems to me the problem?" I asked.

"Well, I saw you hit that cat back there. Don't you think you should at least try to see who the owner is?"

Shit, I'm thinking but thought it's best to do just what he asks then get on my way. "Okay." I said. "I'll do the best I can." So I look around and there are only two houses there. I went up the driveway of the closest one and knocked on the door. A child answers the door. Great, I thought. I've got to tell him I just killed his pet.

"Is your mother home?" I asked, and the little boy gave me a cautious look then went and got his mother. She comes to the door and the little boy is standing next to her so I ask, "Do you own a cat?" To my surprise, the mother says no. She tells me to go to the other house where a little old lady lives who owns a bunch of cats.

As I come down the driveway, the police officer is waiting there. I tell him about the little kid and his mom and yes, I went to the other house which had a long curving driveway. I get to the house and there's a little old lady standing outside calling for "Patches, Patches?"

Oh Shit! I thought. This is getting really bad. Then said, "Excuse me M'am do you own a black cat?"

She looks into my eyes and says, "Yes, I own a black cat called 'Patches'".

So I tell her the whole story on how I accidently killed her cat and told her how sorry I was. When the whole ordeal was over, I headed back down the driveway and the police officer is still waiting there. So I tell him what happened, and then asked if I could be on my way.

"Don't you think you should offer her some money for killing her cat?" He replied.

I was getting pissed and just wanted to get this over with. I looked in my wallet and only had a $20 bill that I needed for lunch. But this was just getting too complicated so I went back up the driveway and apologized again to her and offered her my last $20. She took it eagerly which again pissed me off but at least it was over and I started back down the driveway.

As I'm walking down the long curving driveway, two police cars with their lights flashing come barreling up the driveway past me and put the old lady under arrest. What the fuck? I'm thinking. I'm flabbergasted so I asked one of the policemen what the hell was going on.

"Simple," he said. "She's being arrested for selling pussy."

"You buy a hat like this; I bet you get a free bowl of soup.... Oh, it looks good on you though."

-Rodney Dangerfield, Caddyshack

Three guys are waiting at the golf course for their fourth player whose name was Hung Lo. Hung Lo worked for one of them. Hung's boss calls Hung Lo on his mobile and says, "Why you late Hung?"

"Hey, boss I not come golf today, I reary sick. I got headache, stomach ache, my arms hurt. I not come golf."

The boss says, "You know Hung, I reary need you today. We're playing foursomes and you're the best golfer at my company. When I feel like this I go to my wife and tell her give me sex. Makes everything better and I can go to golf. You try."

127

An hour later Hung still isn't there. His boss gets on the mobile again and calls Hung and asks where he is.

"Boss, I do what you say and I feel great. I be at golf soon. You got nice house."

"V. J. Singh hits more balls than Elton John's chin."

-David Feherty

A gorgeous young lady golfer was beginning a practice round by herself early on a summer's evening. The assistant golf pro who was cleaning golf carts noticed her and quickly reached into his pocket and put on his new watch, grabbed his clubs, and walked up to the first tee and asked if he could join her.

"Sure, not a problem, I might get some golf tips as well from you if you don't mind?"

The young golf pro smiled and nodded yes to her question. As they played a few holes the young lady noticed the watch on his hand. "Is that one of the new distance measuring GPS watches?

"No, it's a watch," the young pro said.

"But it has a blank face, it's all white, how can you tell the time?"

"Oh it's one of those new telepathic psychic watches which transmit the time to me telepathically. It also tells me things."

The gorgeous young woman golfer was wide eyed. "Wow that's amazing! What does it tell you?"

The young pro looked at his watch and studied it for a few seconds. Then he said, "Well it tells me you're not wearing any underpants."

She was amazed at his guess but smiled assuredly and then said, "You're wrong, I am wearing underpants."

The pro now puzzled, looked at his watch again and shook his wrist. Then he held it up to his ear, then cleaned the front of it and shook it again and said, "Oh, it's running about an hour fast."

"The missus asked me, 'When you're on a guy's only golf trip, do you think about me?'

"Apparently, 'Only to stop myself from coming too quickly,' wasn't the right answer."

-Author unknown

The country club announced in their newsletter that Bubba the caddy decided to move on and would be leaving the club. Most of the lady members were saddened by the news. Bubba received many thank you cards and as he was leaving on his last day, one lady member invited him to have lunch at her home.

Bubba happily accepted. After lunch, the lady member invited him up to the bedroom for some "desert" which he gladly and eagerly accepted again.

They have ravishing sex in the bedroom but when they were finished, the lady member handed a dollar to Bubba.

"What's the dollar for?" asked Bubba.

"It was my husband's suggestion. When I told him you were leaving I asked him if we should get you something for the years you worked at the Club, and he told me 'Fuck him, give him a dollar.' The lunch was my idea."

"I don't care to join any club that's prepared to have me as a member."

-Groucho Marx

Two men played golf together frequently. One was several strokes better than the other. The lesser player was very proud, and never wanted to take any strokes to even up the game.

One Saturday morning, the lesser player shows up with a gorilla at the first tee. He says to his friend, "I've been trying to beat you for so long that I'm about ready to give up. But, I heard about this golfing gorilla, and I was wondering if it would be alright if he plays for me today? In fact if you're game, I'd like to try to get back all the money I've lost to you this year. I figure comes to about a thousand bucks. Are you willing?"

The other guy thought about it for a minute, and then decided to play the gorilla. "After all, how good could a gorilla be at golf?" he thought.

Well, the first hole was a straightaway par 4 of 450 yards. The guy hits a beautiful tee shot, 275 yards down the middle, leaving himself a 6 iron to the green. The gorilla takes a few powerful practice swings and then laces the ball 450 yards, right at the pin, stopping about 6 inches away from the hole.

The guy turns to his friend and says "That's incredible, I would have never believed it if I hadn't seen it with my own eyes. But, you know what? I've seen enough! I've got no interest in being totally humiliated by this gorilla golfing machine. You send this fuckin' gorilla back to where he comes from! I need a drink; better make it a double, and I'll write you a check."

After handing over the check, and well into his second double the guy asks, "By the way, how's that gorilla's putting?"

The other guy replies, "Same as his driving."
"That good, huh?"

"No, I mean, he hits putts the same way - 450 yards, right down the middle!"

"Fortunately, he (Rory McIlroy) is 22 years old so his right wrist should be the strongest muscle in his body."

-David Feherty

Two lesbians were out playing golf. They tee off and one drive goes to the right and one drive goes to the left. One of them finds her ball in a patch of buttercups. She grabs a club and takes a mighty swing at the ball. She hits a beautiful second shot, but in the process she hacks the hell out of the buttercups.

Suddenly a gorgeous woman appears out of a puff of smoke - out of nowhere! She blocks her path to her golf bag and stares at her and says, "I'm Mother Nature, and I don't like the way you treated my buttercups. From now on, you won't be able to stand the taste of butter. Each time you eat butter you will become physically ill to the point of total nausea."

Mother Nature disappears as quickly as she appeared. Shaken, the woman calls out to her partner, "Hey, where's your ball?"

"It's over here in the pussy willows."

"I get no respect. I was such an ugly kid, when I played in the sandbox; the cat kept covering me up."

-Rodney Dangerfield

Three very handsome male dogs, a black lab belonging to Jordan Spieth, a golden retriever belonging to Bubba Watson, and a Mexican Chihuahua belonging to Lee Trevino are walking down the street when they see a beautiful, enticing, female Poodle. All three dogs fall all over themselves in an effort to be the one to reach her first, but end up arriving in front of her at the same time. The males are speechless before her beauty, slobbering on themselves and hoping for just a glance from her in return.

Aware of her charms and her obvious effect on the three suitors, she decides to be kind and tells them "The first one who can use the words "liver" and "cheese" together in an imaginative, intelligent sentence can fuck me."

The sturdy, muscular black Lab speaks up quickly and says "I love liver and cheese."

"Oh, how childish," said the Poodle. "That shows no imagination or intelligence whatsoever."

She turned to the tall, shiny Golden Retriever and said "How well can you do?"

"Ummmm...I hate liver and cheese," blurts the Golden Retriever."

"My, my," said the Poodle. "I guess it's hopeless. That's just as dumb as the Lab's sentence." She then turns to the last of the three dogs and says, "How about you, little guy?"

The last of the three, tiny in stature but big in his heart and finesse, is the Mexican Chihuahua. He gives her a smile, a sly wink, turns to the Golden Retriever and the Lab and says... "Liver alone. Cheese mine."

"Never bet with anyone you meet on the first tee who has a deep suntan, a one iron in his bag and has squinty eyes."

-Dave Marr

A Mexican golfer who doesn't speak English very well checks into the posh Golf Resort in Florida. He's standing at the check-in while the clerk processes his registration.

The desk clerk looks up and asks, "Senor, how many sheets do you want on your bed?"

The Mexican blankly stares at the clerk awhile and then says, "If you sheet on my bed man, I think I'll kill you, no?"

"So I jump ship in Hong Kong and make my way over to Tibet, and I get on as looper at a course over in the Himalayas.

"A looper?

"You know a caddy, a looper, a jock. So I tell 'em I'm a pro jock, and who do you think they give me? The Dalai Lama himself. The 12th son of the Lama. The flowing robes, the grace, bald... striking.

"So, I'm on the first tee with him. I give him the driver. He hauls off and whacks one—big hitter, the Lama—looong, into a 10,000-foot crevasse right at the base of this glacier.

"Do you know what the Lama says? Gunga galunga... gunga, gunga-galunga.

"So we finish the 18th and he's gonna stiff me. And I say, 'Hey, Lama, hey, how about a little something, you know, for the effort, you know?'

"And he says, 'Oh, uh, there won't be any money, but when you die, on your deathbed, you will receive total consciousness.' So I got that goin' for me, which is nice."

-Bill Murray, Caddyshack

"One of the most fascinating things about golf is how it reflects the cycle of life. No matter what you shoot, you have to go back to the first tee the next day and begin all over again and make yourself into something."

-Peter Jacobsen

A man takes the day off work and decides to go out golfing. He is on the second hole when he notices a frog sitting next to the green. He thinks nothing of it and is about to shoot when he hears, "Ribbit. 9- Iron". The man looks around and doesn't see anyone. "Ribbit. 9-Iron." He looks at the frog and decides to prove the frog wrong. He puts his other club away, and grabs a 9-iron. Boom! He hits it 10 inches from the cup. He is shocked!

He says to the frog, "Wow that's amazing. You must be a lucky frog, eh?"

The frog replies "Ribbit. Lucky frog."

The man decides to take the frog with him to the next hole a 220 yard par 3. "What do you think frog?" the man asks.

"Ribbit. 3-wood." The guy takes out a 3-wood, and boom! A hole in one. The man is befuddled and doesn't know what to say. By the end of the day, the man has golfed the best game of golf in his life and asks the frog, "OK where to next?"

The frog replies, "Ribbit. Las Vegas." They go to Las Vegas and the guy says, "OK frog, now what?"

The frog says, "Ribbit. Roulette."

Upon approaching the roulette table, the man asks, "What do you think I should bet?"

The frog replies, "Ribbit. $10,000, black 6."

Now, this is a risky with a very slim chance to win, but after the golf game, the man figures what the hell. Boom – piles and piles of chips come sliding back across the table. The man takes his winnings and buys the best room in the hotel. He sits the frog down and says, "Frog, I don't know how to repay you. You've won me all this money and I am forever grateful."

The frog replies, "Ribbit, Kiss Me."

He figures, Why not? After all the frog did for him, it is a small price to pay. With the kiss, however, the frog turns into a gorgeous 17-year-old girl.

"And that, your honor, is how the girl ended up in my room."

"An endless series of tragedies obscured by the occasional miracle."

-Anonymous

An American golfer just finished playing the famous links course at Royal Dornach in Northern Scotland and was exhausted from his round. He was use to riding in a cart when he played golf since he had a bad knee and was a bit overweight. This time, however, he walked the course and carried his clubs like the old Scottish golfers in order to enjoy a pure experience.

While playing the seaside links, he saw an elderly man standing a bit off the fairway, then lost his balance and fell into the cold ocean. He jumped off the cliff into the freezing waters and saved the old man. Then finished his round avoiding a crowd gathering to thank him for his valour.

He finished his round and could hardly stand up as he boarded a train taking him back to his hotel. The train was very crowded, so the tired hero walked the length of the train, looking for an empty seat. The only unoccupied seat was directly adjacent to a well-dressed middle-aged lady and the last seat left was being used by her little dog. The weary golfer asked, "Please, ma'am, would you kindly allow me to sit in that seat?"

The English woman looked down her nose at the golfer, sniffed and said, "You Americans. You are such a rude class of people. Can't you see my little Twinkie is using that seat?" The golfer walked away, determined to find a place to rest, but after another trip down to the end of the train, found himself again facing the woman with the dog.

Again he asked, "Please, lady. May I sit there? I'm sorry but I'm very tired and my knee is killing me."

The English woman wrinkled her nose and snorted, "You Americans! Not only are you rude, you are also arrogant. Imagine!"

The golfer didn't say anything else; he leaned over, picked up the little dog, tossed it out the window of the train and sat down in the empty seat. The woman shrieked and railed, and demanded that someone defend her and chastise the golfer.

An English gentleman who had also finished a golf round was sitting across the aisle spoke up, "You know, sir, you Americans do seem to have a penchant for doing the wrong thing. You eat holding the fork in the wrong hand. You drive your cars on the wrong side of the road. And now, sir, you've thrown the wrong bitch out the window."

6. BIG DICK GOLF JOKES

A golfer was shaving in the locker room after a round, when his caddie, Bubba, walked in to take a piss. The golfer couldn't help but notice when Bubba took his dick out it was huge. Bubba finished and was washing his hands, when the golfer asked, "Bubba, I'll bet the girls like that one eyed python of yours?"

"Yeah, keeps me busy," replied Bubba.

"Bubba, what's your secret to getting a big dick?"

Bubba replied, "Well, every night before I go to get in bed with a woman, I whack my dick on the bedpost three times."

So the golfer decides to try it that very night. He came in late and his wife was asleep. Right before the golfer got into bed, he whacked his

Absolutely Hilarious Adult Golf Joke Book

dick on the bedpost three times and his wife woke up and said, "Bubba, is that you?"

"Of course I talk to myself. Sometimes I need an expert opinion."

-Bill Murray, Caddyshack

A golfer walks into the clubhouse bar and sits down and orders a drink. He notices a jar full of money resting on the bar in front of him. The golfer asks the bartender what the jar is for. The bartender then says, "I have a donkey in the back room and if anyone can make him laugh they win the money in the jar. If not they owe me 100 dollars."

The golfer says "I can do it!" The golfer goes into the back room and about 5 minutes later the bartender hears the donkey roaring out loud with laughter. The golfer walks out and takes the money from the jar, thanks the bartender, and leaves.

About a month later the same golfer comes back into the clubhouse bar and there is a new jar full of money and the golfer asks the bartender what the new jar of money is for.

The bartender looks at the golfer and says, "If you can make the donkey cry the money is yours, if not you owe me 100 dollars."

The golfer says, "Okay I'll do it!" The golfer walks into the back room and after about 2 minutes, the bartender hears the donkey sobbing away uncontrollably. The golfer walks out and grabs the money out of the jar.

The bartender asks, "How did you make the donkey laugh?" The golfer looks at the bartender and says, "Well the first time I told the donkey that I had a bigger dick then he did".

"Then, how did you make him cry?" asked the bartender?

"Well I showed him."

*

That same golfer took his 5 year old son to the 43 acre Animal Kingdom Lodge at Disney World wanting to see elephants in their natural habitat.

The small boy watched the elephants roam with giraffes in high grasses. The high grass gave one large male elephant an erection and the small boy pointed to it and asked, "What's that?"

The golfer replied, "That is the elephant's penis."

The little boy was confused and said, "When mom brought me here, she told me it was 'nothing'".

The golfer smiled and simply said, "Your mother's spoiled."

"It takes longer to learn to be a good golfer than it does to become a brain surgeon. On the other hand, you don't get to ride around on a cart, drink beer, eat hot dogs and stare at the cart girl's tits all day if you are performing brain surgery."

-Unknown doctor

A young golfer was hitting balls on a range trying to get the attention of Gary Player who was hitting on the other side of the range. Every time Gary Player would hit a ball the young golfer hit if further then looked at Gary to see if he impressed him.

Gary would hit a fade then the young golfer hit a picturesque fade even further and so on. This started to annoy Gary and waved the young golfer over to him.

"You hit some impressive shots for a youngster. I was wondering if you've got your tour card yet."

"Well I could get it any time, I was leading in the last three qualifiers but thought, hey, it's too easy. All that travel? Nah, not for me yet, even though I could qualify any time I choose. I'm going to have fun before I get into that grind."

Player stared at him, and then said, "You know I've designed over three hundred golf courses, and I could get you a job at one of the most exclusive courses I've ever designed. They pay around $100k for a new assistant pro and the course is owned by a very wealthy old man who also wants a chauffeur and a bodyguard for his beautiful daughter and you'll have to see to all of her needs. You're young and very tall and I assume you got a dick because from what I hear, and I don't mean to be awkward but, you're going to need it with this job."

"Yeah, yeah, I got a dick," said the young golfer, now getting really excited.

"Well you'll have to fly over to South Africa to meet everyone but the owner will send his jet for you and his daughter will come to meet you. She's in her early 20s and she's got one hell of a sex drive. Oh, and you'll have to escort her on all her trips," said Gary.

The young golfer, now wide-eyed, said, "You bullshittin' me!"

Gary replied, "Yeah, well….You started it…."

"The sport of choice for the urban poor is basketball. The sport of choice for maintenance level employees is bowling. The sport of choice for front–line workers is football. The sport of choice for supervisors is baseball. The sport of choice for middle management is tennis. The sport of choice for corporate officers is golf. Therefore, the higher up you are in the corporate structure the smaller your balls become."

-Unknown

Three golfers stopped at a supermarket to pick up some things they needed for a weekend golf trip. When the first one got to the register he realized he had forgotten to get condoms, so he asked the checkout girl if she could have some brought up to the register. She asked, "What size condoms?"

The customer replied he didn't know.

She asked him to drop his pants. He did. She reached over the counter, grabbed his dick and called over the intercom, "One box of large condoms, Register 5."

His buddy was next in line and thought this was interesting, and like most of us, was up for a cheap thrill. When he got to the register he told the check out girl that he too forgot a box of condoms. She asked him what size and he didn't know so she asked him to drop his pants and she reached over and grabbed his dick and called over the intercom, "One box of medium sized condoms, Register 5."

The third golf in the group had just turned 21 and was still a virgin and thought what he'd just seen was very cool. He hadn't had any sexual contact with a live female, so this was a golden opportunity for him. She asked him what size and he didn't know. She asked him to drop his pants and he did. She reached over the counter, gave him a quick squeeze then picked up the intercom and said, "Clean up, Register 5."

"How did I make a twelve on a par 5 hole? It's simple. I missed a four foot putt for an eleven."

-Arnold Palmer

A golfer was going away on a business trip with a business group for a golf travel adventure for two weeks. He knew his wife was a flirtatious sort, so he thought he'd try to get her something to keep her occupied while he was gone, because he didn't much like the idea of her screwing someone else.

So he went to a store that sold sex toys and started looking around. He thought about a life-sized sex doll, but that was too close to another man for him. He was browsing through the dildos, looking for something special to please his wife, and started talking to the old man behind the counter. He explained his situation to the old man.

"Well, I don't really know of anything that will do the trick. We have vibrating dildos, special attachments, and so on, but I don't know of anything that will keep her occupied for two weeks, except …" said the old man, and then he stopped.

"Except what," asked the businessman?

"Nothing, nothing," said the old man.

"C'mon, tell me! I need something!" protested the businessman.

"Well, sir, I don't usually mention this, but there is the 'Voodoo Dick,'" the old man said.

"So what's up with this Voodoo Dick," the businessman asked? The old man reached under the counter, and pulled out an ancient wooden box carved with strange symbols. He opened it, and there lay a very ordinary-looking dildo. The businessman laughed, and said, "Big fucking deal. It looks like every other dildo in this shop!"

The old man said, "But you haven't seen what it'll do yet." He pointed to a door and said "Voodoo dick, the door." The voodoo dick rose out of its box, darted over to the door, and started screwing the keyhole. The whole door shook with the vibrations, and a crack developed down the middle.

Before the door could split, the old man said, "Voodoo dick, get back in your box!" The voodoo dick stopped, floated back to the box and lay there, quiescent once more.

The businessman said, "I'll take it!" The old man resisted and said it wasn't for sale, but he finally surrendered to $2,000 in cash. The guy took it home to his wife, told her it was a special dildo and that to use it, all she had to do was say, "Voodoo dick, my pussy."

He left for his trip satisfied things would be fine while he was gone. After he'd been gone a few days, the wife was unbearably horny. She thought of several people who would willingly satisfy her, but then she remembered the voodoo dick. She got it out, and said "Voodoo dick, my pussy!"

The voodoo dick shot to her crotch and started pumping. It was great, like nothing she'd ever experienced before. After three orgasms, she decided she'd had enough, and tried to pull it out, but it was stuck in her, still thrusting. She tried and tried to get it out, but nothing worked. Her husband had forgotten to tell her how to shut it off. So she decided to go to the hospital to see if they could help. She put her clothes on, got in the car and started to drive to the hospital, quivering with every thrust of the dildo.

On the way, another orgasm nearly made her swerve off the road, and she was pulled over by a policeman.

He asked for her license, and then asked how much she'd had to drink. Gasping and twitching, she explained that she hadn't been drinking but a voodoo dick was in her pussy and wouldn't stop screwing her, and that's why she swerved all over the road.

The officer looked at her for a second, and then said, "Yea, right. Voodoo dick, my ass!"

"It's just a glorious day. The only way to ruin a day like this would be to play golf on it."

-David Feherty

A very polite golfer is checking in at a famous Orlando, Florida Golf Resort in the lobby. After he checks in, he rushes to the men's locker room trying to still make his tee time. As he rushes, he accidentally bumps into a woman standing nearby and as he does, his elbow rubs repeatedly over her breast.

Startled and ashamed, the golfer says, "Ma'am, if your heart is as soft as your breast, I know you'll forgive me."

She replies, "If your fuckin' dick is as hard as your elbow, I'm in room 1221."

"When I die, bury me on a golf course so my husband will visit me."

-Anonymous

Tell your golf buddies about Noah's ark:

It's day 3 on Noah's ark, and the animals could no longer hold their sexual desire, so they started having sex with one another. Noah's pissed off since the grinding made the Ark shake dangerously and he decided that it was time to put things in order. So he ordered that every male should get a card stating the name of his wife and the days they were allowed to mate.

So they did... After a couple of days, during breakfast in the Ark's cafeteria the monkey said to his wife: "You'd better get ready because next Tuesday you'll get the really big one and it will hurt so good -- you'll suffer baby!"

The female monkey felt really ashamed because all of the animals heard her husband… The day after, the male monkey said to his wife again: "Oh baby! You'd better get ready and do your stretching 'because next Tuesday you'll suffer cruelly!" The female monkey told Noah what had happened, so Noah called the male monkey in his office and asked for an explanation.

"You stinking kinky monkey! Why do you disgrace your wife in front of all the other animals?" said Noah.

"I am not kinky sir", said the monkey "I'm just trying to get her ready and warning her because I lost my sex card in a golf match with the elephant and now he has it…."

7. ABSOLUTELY HILARIOUS GOLF JOKES

"No one will ever have golf under his thumb. No round ever will be so good it could not have been better.   Perhaps this is why golf is the greatest of all games. You are not playing a human adversary; you are playing a game. You are playing old man par."

-Bobby Jones

A New Yorker and a Texan, both high handicappers, were spraying their shots resulting in the Texan driving and bouncing the cart through very rough tough terrain trying to find their golf balls. It got so bumpy the New Yorker hit his head on the cart's roof then fell out of the cart.

"Hey, take it easy partner. This ain't a rodeo," the New Yorker said as he got up rubbing his head.

"Shit, pardner, you ought to learn bronc riding," said the Texan.

The New Yorker said, "Sounds great but there's no rodeos in the Big Apple."

"You don't need a rodeo. Just get your girlfriend down on all fours and mount her from behind. Then reach round and cup both of her breast and whisper, 'Your sister has bigger ones', then try to hold on for eight seconds!"

"It took me seventeen years to get three thousand hits in baseball. It took one afternoon on the golf course."

-Hank Aaron

Two golfers are having a round on a golf course in the Canadian woods. One golfer goes into the dense brush looking for his ball and spots a very large bear. He violently swings his golf club at the bear and the bear disappears.

An instant later, the bear taps the hunter on the shoulder and says, "No one swings a club at me and gets away with it. You have two choices: I can rip your throat out and eat you, or you can drop your trousers, bend over, and I'll have my way with you." The golfer decides that anything is better than death, so he drops his trousers and bends over; and the bear pounds away at him.

After the bear has left, the golfer pulls up his trousers and staggers back into town. He's pretty mad. He gets his rifle and returns to the forest. He sees the same bear, aims, and fires. When the smoke clears, the bear is gone.

An instant later the bear taps the golfer on the shoulder and says, "You know what to do."

Afterward, the golfer pulls up his trousers, crawls back into town, and buys a missile launcher. Now he's really mad. He returns to the forest, sees the bear, aims, and fires. The force of the missile blast knocks him flat on his back. When the smoke clears, the bear is standing over him and says, "You're not doing this for the golf, are you?"

I saw a fortune teller the other day. She told me I would come into some money. Last night I fucked a girl named Penny. Is that spooky or what?"

-unknown

A couple was arguing. The dad had come home late from golf and she was furious he'd forgotten her mother's birthday party that day. He repeatedly apologized, but the argument continued. The dad, frustrated, called the mom a "bitch" and the mom called the dad a "bastard". Their small son walked in and said "What does bitch and bastard mean?" and the couple said, "ladies and gentlemen".

The next day the couple were having sex, the mom said "feel my tits" and the dad said "feel my cock". Their son walked in and asked "What does tits and cock mean?" and the couple replied "hats and coats".

On Thanksgiving the dad was shaving and he cut himself, "Shit" he said, the kid came in and asked "What's that mean" and the dad said it was the brand shaving cream he was using.

Downstairs the mom was preparing the turkey, and she cut herself, "Fuck" she said. Once again the kid asked "What's that mean" the mom said that is what she calls stuffing the turkey.

Then the door bell rang. The kid answered the door to his uncle and aunt and other relatives and said, "Alright you bitches and bastards, put your dicks and tits in the closet, my dad is upstairs wiping the shit off his face, and my mom is in the kitchen fucking the turkey!

"Professional golf is the only sport where if you win 20% of the time, you're the best."

-Jack Nicklaus

A young assistant pro and his girl friend were riding in a golf cart at the end of the day over a deserted golf course. The young pro decided to show off his driving skills as he zig-zagged around the course. His girlfriend was thrilled at this driving. So the pro suggested, "If I do a 360 degree spin with this cart, will you take off your clothes?"

"Yes!" said his girlfriend.

He does a magnificent spin. She peels off all her clothes. He continued showing off, speeding the cart to its limit, but he couldn't keep his eyes ahead, and the cart skidded and slipped on loose gravel making the cart flip over. His naked girlfriend was thrown clear, but he was jammed beneath the steering wheel.

"Go and get help!" he cried.

"But I can't. I'm naked and my clothes are gone!"

"Take my shoe", he said, "and cover yourself."

Holding the shoe over her pussy, the girl ran down the road and found a fire station. Still holding the shoe between her legs, she ran in and pleaded to the first fireman she saw, "Please help me! My boyfriend's stuck!"

The fireman glanced at the shoe and said, "There's nothing I can do...he's in too far."

"I'm fed up with the excuses women come up with to avoid having sex, like: 'I'm tired.' I'm washing my hair. I've got a headache. I am your sister-in-law.'"

-unknown

A husband and wife were playing golf in the early evening when the husband hit his ball into a water hazard. Trying to get his ball, he fell in the water. He staggered out, all wet and muddy and his sympathetic wife reached in her bag and gave him a clean towel. As he dried himself, he looked at her with his eyes filled with tears.

"You know what? You've been with me over the years through all the bad times. Remember when I kept getting fired, you always supported me. When my business failed, you were there. When I got robbed and shot, you were by my side. When we lost the house, you stayed right here. When my health started failing, you were still by my side. You know what?"

"What dear?" she asked gently, smiling as her heart began to fill with warmth.

The husband flings the towel back at her and says, "I think you're fuckin' bad luck."

"I'm aware that if I'm playing at my best, I'm tough to beat. I enjoy that."

-Tiger Woods

A golfer who was never home since he was working and playing too much golf was suspicious of his wife cheating on him and wanted to catch her in the act. He couldn't afford a private investigator so he went to a pet shop.

At the pet shop he asks the clerk if he has a parrot for sale. The clerk shows him the last parrot he has: "This is the last parrot I have for sale. He doesn't have any legs, but he is very smart."

The man asks, "If he doesn't have any legs, how does he stay on the perch?"

"He holds on with his dick." the clerk answered.

The man asks, "How much?"

"Since the parrot doesn't have any legs, I'll sell him to you for fifty bucks."

The suspicious man purchases the talking bird and takes him home. He sets up the cage in his bedroom where the parrot can see everything and instructs the parrot to watch what ever goes on in the room and inform him when he gets home from work.

So the next morning he leaves for work and his wife stays home, as usual. When the man gets home from work, as his wife is cooking supper, he asks the parrot to tell him what went on during the day. The parrot begins, "At eight o'clock this morning the mailman came...."

Interrupting, the man asks, "Yeah and what happened?"

"He came in the house –"

Furiously, the golfer asked "And then?"

"And he came into the bedroom –"

Astounded the man impatiently asks, "What happened next?"

"He began to take off his clothes and she hers – "

"What happened after that?"

The parrot then replied, "I don't know I got a boner and fell off the fuckin' perch!"

"My wife just came in and said, "I don't know if I'm coming or going."

So I said to her, "Judging by the look on your face you're going, because when you're coming you look like a fucking squirrel trying to whistle!"

-unknown

A golfer's wife was a bit irate he preferred golf over her each Saturday but got use to it after awhile. They rarely had sex and the husband just finished making love quickly on a Saturday morning, and then jumped up to shower rushing to make his tee time. The wife remarked, "Oh another wham bam thank you M'am?"

"Honey you know I've got the usual game this morning and am trying to make the tee time. I'll make it up to you tomorrow morning," replied the husband.

The wife jumped up and started to pack her suitcase. "Honey what are you doing," said the husband?

"I'm moving to Las Vegas. I could get $200 for what I just did for you for free."

The husband stopped in his rush and grabbed a suitcase and started packing himself. "Hey! I'm the one going to Vegas," said the wife.

The husband continued to pack. "I'm following you to Vegas," the husband said, "I've got to see you live off of $600 a year!"

"Golf is the closest game to the game we call life. You get bad breaks from good shots; you get good breaks from bad shots - but you have to play the ball where it lies."

-Bobby Jones

David was an obsessive golfer and practiced every day, watched the latest instructional videos, and used the most expensive clubs custom fit for him by the golf pro at his club. But his handicap never went down and in fact gradually increased as he practiced harder every day despite his increased frustration and dedication. Sometimes he'd almost have a prefect round then play terribly on the last 5 or 6 holes like a total beginner.

He finally went nuts and absolutely crazy but had sense enough to admit himself to a mental institution. He told the doctor there, "Bad golf actually does make you fuckin' crazy!"

He convalesced for awhile, and then began to practice at the aqua driving range every day at the mental institution. He's hit floating golf balls into a lake and the staff would periodically retrieve the floating balls.

But another patient, John, saw him hitting balls into the water and pushed David down, then ran and dove in the water shouting, "Save the balls, save the balls!"

Well David lost it and began stomping on the ground throwing his golf clubs in every direction. Then he looked up and stared at John struggling in the water going under several times. He realized John was drowning. David instinctively jumped in and saved him. When the medical director came to know of David's heroic act, he called David into his office:

Doctor: "We have good news and bad news for you.

David: The good news is that we are going to discharge you because you have regained your senses. You are a normal person now since you jumped in and risked your own life to save another patient. Congratulations, David."

David: "So what's the bad news?"

Doctor: "The bad news is that, the patient, John, whom you have saved, hung himself in the toilet, and died."

David: "Doctor, he didn't hang himself. I hung him there to dry."

"No matter how bad your last shot was, the worst is yet to come. This law does not expire on the 18th hole, since it has the supernatural tendency to extend over the course of a tournament, a summer and, eventually, a lifetime."

-Unknown

Self punishment for playing bad golf isn't good and may turn you into a masochist:

A masochist golfer, a sadist, a murderer, a necrophile, a zoophile and a pyromaniac are all sitting on a bench by the aqua driving range at the mental institution and they begin to have a discussion:

"Let's have sex with a cat?" asked the zoophile.

"Let's have sex with the cat and then torture it," says the sadist.

"Let's have sex with the cat, torture it and then kill it," shouted the murderer.

"Let's have sex with the cat, torture it, kill it and then have sex with it again," said the necrophile.

"Let's have sex with the cat, torture it, kill it, have sex with it again and then burn it," said the pyromaniac.

There was silence, and then the masochist said: "Meow."

"If you're stupid enough to whiff, you should be smart enough to forget it."

-Arnold Palmer

A nun and a priest decide to take a day off, so they go golfing. The nun is a much better golfer than the priest and on the sixth hole, a par 3, the nun gets a hole-in-one. The priest hits it into a sand trap. He's so angry and jealous, he shouts "God dammit, I fuckin' missed!"

The nun reminds him not to take the Lord's name in vain, and the priest apologizes. On his next tee shot, he hits it into the lake, and in his anger, shouts "God dammit, I MISSED!"

The nun once again tells him not to take the Lord's name in vain, and he apologizes again.

On his next tee shot, he dribbles it off the tee and doesn't even hit it past the ladies tee and yells "GOD DAMMIT I MISSED!" The nun is standing near the ladies tee but before the nun can say anything, a bolt of lightning strikes the nun, killing her instantly.

Out of nowhere, a loud voice booms "God dammit, I missed."

"What brings you to this nape of the woods, neck of the wape, How come you're here?"

"I bet you have a lot of nice ties."

   -Ty Webb and Lacey Underall, Caddyshack

A boss and his secretary are playing golf and the secretary is brilliantly putting – almost one putting every green. She bends down repeatedly showing her shapely ass to her boss taking the ball out of the hole then teeing it up on the next tee.

On the 17th tee, the boss can't take it any longer and says, "I want to have SEX with you. I will make it very fast and worth your while. I'll throw $1,000 down in those bushes over there and by the time you bend down to pick it I'll be done."

The secretary pondered it. She got on her cell phone and called her boyfriend and told him the story. Her boyfriend then said to her, "Do it but ask him for $2,000, pick up the money very fast - he won't even have enough time to undress himself."

So she agrees. Half an hour goes by, the boyfriend decides to call girlfriend. He hears rhythmic thumping in the background and he asks, "What happened?"

She responds trying to catch her breath "The Bastard used coins I'm still picking and he is still fucking!"

"When it comes to putters, try before you buy: Never buy a putter until you've had a chance to throw it."

-unknown

A housewife takes a lover during the day, while her husband is at work. She wasn't aware that her 10 year old son was hiding in the closet. Her husband came home unexpectedly, so she hid her lover in the same closet. The boy now has company.

Boy: "Dark in here."

Man: "Yes it is."

Boy: "I have a golf ball."

Man: "That's nice."

Boy: "Want to buy it?"

Man: "No, thanks."

Boy: "My dad's outside."

Man: "OK, how much?"

Boy: "$250."

In the next few weeks, it happens again that the boy and the mom's lover are in the closet together.

Boy: "Dark in here."

Man: "Yes, it is."

Boy: "I have a pitching wedge."

Man: "That's nice."

Boy: "Want to buy it?"

Man: "No, thanks."

Boy: "I'll tell."

Man: "How much?"

Boy: "$750."

Man: "Fine."

A few days later, the father says to the boy, "Grab your pitching wedge and a ball, let's go outside and practice chipping."

The boy says, "I can't. I sold them."

The father asks, "How much did you sell them for?" The son says, "$1,000."

The father says, "That's terrible to over-charge your friends like that. That's way more than those two things cost. I'm going to take you to church and make you confess."

They go to church and the father alerts the priest and makes the little boy sit in the confession booth and closes the door. The boy says, "Dark in here."

The priest says, "Don't start that shit again."

"When I asked you if you wanted to play around, I didn't mean golf.

-unknown

A man bought a Lie detector robot that slaps people who lie. He decided to test it at dinner.

DAD: I shot a 79 today at the golf course (robot slaps Dad). Okay, I shot a 99.

DAD: Son where were you today during school hours?

SON: At school (Robot slaps the Son) and he immediately changes his mind. Okay I went to the movies.

DAD: Which one?

SON: Harry Potter (Robot slaps Son again!) Okay I was watching porno.

DAD: What? When I was your age I didn't even know what porn was! (Robot slaps dad)

MOM: Haha! After all he is your Son! (Robot gives Mom a slap).

"The best engine in the world is the vagina. It can be started with one finger. It is self lubricating. It takes any size piston and it changes its own oil every 4 weeks. It is a pity though that its management is so fucking temperamental."

-George Carlin

One day a young man and woman were playing golf and all of a sudden a bumble bee passes by the wife and flies up her skirt and into her vagina. The young woman started screaming "Oh my god, help me, there's a bee in my vagina!"

The husband immediately took her to the emergency room and explained the situation to the doctor. The doctor thought for a moment and said "Hmm, tricky situation. But I have a solution to the problem if you would permit me young man?"

The husband being very concerned agreed that the doctor could use whatever method to get the bee out of his wife's vagina. The doctor said "OK, what I'm gonna do is rub some honey over the top of my penis and insert it into your wife's vagina. When I feel the bee getting closer to the tip of my penis I shall withdraw it and the bee should hopefully follow my penis out of your wife's vagina. The husband nodded and gave his approval.

The young lady said "Yes, Yes, whatever, just get on with it."

So the doctor, after covering the tip of his penis with honey, inserted it into the young woman's vagina. After a few gentle strokes, the doctor said, "I don't think the bee has noticed the honey yet. Perhaps I should go a bit deeper." So the doctor went deeper and deeper. After a while the doctor began thrusting the young lady very hard. The young woman began to quiver with excitement. She began to moan and groan aloud. The doctor, concentrating very hard, looked like he was enjoying himself; he then put his hands on the young lady's breasts and started groaning.

The husband at this point suddenly became very annoyed and shouted, "Now wait a minute! What the hell do you think you're doing?"

The doctor, still concentrating, replied, "Change of plan. I'm gonna drown the fuckin' bastard!"

"Dan would rather play golf than have sex any day."

-Marilyn Quayle

Bill worked in a pro shop as assistant pro for two years which has a coffee bar making fresh ground coffee for the golfers.

One day he confesses to his wife that he has a terrible urge to stick his penis into the coffee grinder. His wife suggested he see a therapist to talk about it. Instead Bill vowed to overcome this rash desire on his own. A few weeks later, Bill returned home absolutely ashen.

His wife asks, "What's wrong, Bill?"

"Do you remember how I told you about my tremendous urge to put my penis into the coffee grinder?"

His wife gasps, "My God, Bill, what happened?"

"I got fired."

"No, Bill I mean, what happened with the coffee grinder?"

"Oh, um, she got fired, too."

"If there's a golf course in heaven, I hope it's like Augusta National. I just don't want an early tee time."

-Gary Player

One day Bill was hitting balls at the range and complained to his friend that his elbow really hurt. His friend suggested that he go to a computer at the drug store that can diagnose anything quicker and cheaper than a doctor. "Simply put in a sample of your urine and the computer will diagnose your problem and tell you what you can do about it. It only costs $10."

Bill figured he had nothing to lose, so he filled a jar with his urine sample and went to the drug store. Finding the computer, he poured in the sample and deposited the $10. The computer started making some noise and various lights started flashing. After a brief pause out popped a small slip of paper on which was printed:

"You have tennis elbow. Soak your arm in warm water. Avoid heavy lifting. It will be better in two weeks."

Later that evening while thinking how amazing this new technology was and how it would change medical science forever, he began to wonder if this machine could be fooled. He mixed together some tap water, a stool sample from his dog and urine samples from his wife and daughter. To top it off, he masturbated into the concoction. He went back to the drug store, located the machine, poured in the sample and deposited the $10. The computer again made the usual noise and printed out the following message:

"Your tap water is too hard. Get a water softener. Your dog has worms. Get him vitamins. Your daughter is using cocaine. Put her in a rehabilitation clinic. Your wife is pregnant with twin girls. They aren't yours. Get a lawyer. And if you don't stop jerking off, your tennis elbow will never get better."

"Cheating isn't an accident. Tripping over a tee marker is an accident. But you don't just trip and fall into a vagina."

-unknown

A husband tells his wife he's out golfing on a Saturday with some friends and the wife is at home when she hears someone knocking at her door. She goes to the door opens it and sees a man standing there. He asks the lady, "Do you have a vagina?" She slams the door in disgust.

The husband goes golfing the next day and his wife is at home and she hears a knock at the door, it's the same man and he asks the same question to the woman, "Do you have a vagina?" She slams the door again.

Later that day when her husband gets home from his so called "golf round" she tells him what has happened for the last two days.

The husband tells his wife in a loving and concerned voice, "Honey, I am taking off Monday so I'll be home, just in case this guy shows up again."

The next morning they hear a knock at the door and both ran for the door. The husband whispers to the wife, "Honey, I'm going to hide behind the door and listen and if it's the same guy I want you to answer yes to the question because I want to a see where he's going with this."

She nods "yes" to her husband and opens the door.

Sure enough the same fellow is standing there, he asks, "Do you have a vagina?"

"Yes I do." says the lady.

The man replies, "Good, would you mind telling your husband to leave my wife's alone and start using yours!"

"I never under estimate my opponent, but I never underestimate my talents."

-Hale Irwin

A doctor, an architect, and a pro golfer were dining at the country club after a round, and the conversation turned to the subject of their respective dogs, which were quite extraordinary. They each threw a $100 bill on the table and bet who had the most intelligent dog.

The physician offered to show his dog first, and called to the parking lot, "Hippocrates, come!" Hippocrates ran in, and was told by the doctor to do his stuff.

Hippocrates ran to the golf course and dug for a while, producing a number of bones. He dragged the bones into the country club, and assembled them into a complete, fully articulated human skeleton. The physician patted Hippocrates on the head, and gave him a cookie for his efforts.

The architect was only marginally impressed, and called for his dog, "Sliderule, come!" Sliderule ran in, and was told to do his stuff.

The dog immediately chewed the skeleton to bits, but reassembled the fragments into an exact scale model of the Empire State Building. The architect patted his dog and gave him a cookie.

The pro golfer blankly watched the other two dogs and then yelled, "Bullshit, come!" Bullshit entered and was told to do his stuff.

Bullshit immediately fucked the other two dogs, stole their cookies, and auctioned the Empire State Building replica to the other club members for a fee. The dog then snatched the $100 bills off the table, and gave it to his master who went outside to play golf.

"It's good sportsmanship to not pick up lost golf balls while they are still rolling."

-Mark Twain

A young lady golfer dated a young assistant pro and they got on very well. "You're not like the rest of the women I've met, you've got a lot of class and are so well mannered, and I'd love you to meet my parents," the assistant pro told her.

She goes to her boyfriend's parents' house which turns out to be a huge mansion in the Hamptons for the first time for dinner and she's very nervous. They all sit down and begin eating. The young lady starts to feel a little discomfort, thanks to her nervousness and the broccoli casserole and the severe gas pains soon are making her eyes water. Left with no other choice, she decides to relieve herself a bit and squeaks out a dainty fart.

It wasn't loud, but everyone at the table heard the fluff. Before she even had a chance to be embarrassed, her boyfriend's father looked over at the dog that had been snoozing at the woman's feet and said in a rather stern voice, "Skippy!"

The woman thought, "What a thoughtful man." and a big smile came across her face. A couple of minutes later, she was beginning to feel the pain again. This time, she didn't even hesitate. She let a much louder and longer fart bleep out. The father again looked at Skippy and yelled, "Dammit Skippy!" Once again the woman smiled and thought "How considerate."

A few minutes later the woman had to blow gas again but this time she didn't even think about it. It sounded like 16 trombones and trumpets blaring in a parade!

Once again, the father looked at the dog with disgust and yelled, "Dammit Skippy, get away from her before she fuckin' shits all over you!"

"I spent $35,000 on a boob job for the wife. She was delighted. I spent another $12,000 on a nose job for her. She was ecstatic. I spent $22,000 on liposuction for her and she couldn't thank me enough. But I spend $500 on a blowjob for myself and she goes fucking nuts! Women, I can't figure them out."

-unknown

A foursome was out playing a golf course with a par three hole which featured a live volcano in the South Pacific.

Only three of them finished the round. The club pro came out and asked where Harry was?

One of them sadly said, "He hit it close to the crater. All of a sudden we heard sounds like heavy seas swishing and crashing against the rocks, then a great rumble, then the ground shook, then we heard a great hissing sound, then a large boulder as big as a pickup truck came flying out of the crater about 100 feet right above Harry."

"Didn't he get out of the way," the club pro asked?

"He looked up at the boulder...his last words were, 'What the fuck?'... then the boulder came down and crushed him."

"Shit! I'll get out there right away!"

"Don't bother, we don't need a ruling. The boulder sent his ball flying on the green and into the hole and we already gave him a birdie."

***

Lightning Source UK Ltd.
Milton Keynes UK
UKHW02f0603200918

329215UK00010B/515/P